Rebecca Cross is a specialist family law
Birmingham. In private law proceedings, Rebecca has particular experience in cases involving coercive and controlling behaviour and allegations of parental alienation. She appears at all stages of proceedings and at all levels of court. Rebecca is popular with solicitors and clients in difficult, complex and/or high-conflict long-running private children cases. On a recent reported case the expert psychologist described the proceedings as *'about as acrimonious as they get'*.

Rebecca is ranked as a tier 1 rising star within the Legal 500 2022 guide. She regularly speaks and writes on all aspects of family law to solicitors and other professionals. She also sits on the Young Resolution West Midlands committee.

Malvika Jaganmohan is a specialist family law barrister at St Ives Chambers in Birmingham. Malvika has a busy private law practice, and she has a particular interest in the international movement of children, forced marriage and cases which concern complex and serious allegations of domestic abuse.

Alongside her practice, Malvika is a mental health advocate; she runs a blog called 'Stiff Upper Lip' on mental health and wellbeing in the legal profession, and she is a Champion for LawCare. She has been named a *'legal change-maker'* in Obelisk Support and First 100 Years' 'Class of 2020: Women Who Will'.

Malvika co-hosts a family law podcast, 'Professionally Embarrassing', which has been shortlisted for Family Law Commentator of the Year in the LexisNexis Family Law Awards 2021. She is a founding member of Women in Family Law and she is part of the core group for The Transparency Project, a charity which aims to make family justice clearer for the general public. Malvika was nominated for Young Pro Bono Barrister of the Year in the Bar Pro Bono Awards 2020.

A Practical Guide to Practice Direction 12J and Domestic Abuse in Private Law Children Proceedings

A Practical Guide to Practice Direction 12J and Domestic Abuse in Private Law Children Proceedings

Rebecca Cross

Malvika Jaganmohan

Law Brief Publishing

© Rebecca Cross and Malvika Jaganmohan

All rights reserved. No part of this publication may be reproduced, stored in a retrieval system, or transmitted, in any form or by any means, electronic, mechanical, photocopying, recording or otherwise, without the prior permission of the publisher.

Excerpts from judgments and statutes are Crown copyright. Any Crown Copyright material is reproduced with the permission of the Controller of OPSI and the Queen's Printer for Scotland. Some quotations may be licensed under the terms of the Open Government Licence (http://www.nationalarchives.gov.uk/doc/open-government-licence/version/3).

Cover image © iStockphoto.com/ThomasVogel

The information in this book was believed to be correct at the time of writing. All content is for information purposes only and is not intended as legal advice. No liability is accepted by either the publisher or author for any errors or omissions (whether negligent or not) that it may contain. Professional advice should always be obtained before applying any information to particular circumstances.

Published 2021 by Law Brief Publishing, an imprint of Law Brief Publishing Ltd
30 The Parks
Minehead
Somerset
TA24 8BT

www.lawbriefpublishing.com

Paperback: 978-1-913715-81-6

For all the family lawyers who work tirelessly for their clients in a broken system.

With particular thanks to Dr Julie Doughty and Professor Jo Delahunty QC for their invaluable comments on this text.

FOREWORD

It was striking, in the Court of Appeal, when getting ready to appear in *Re T* in the conjoined cases of *Re H-N and ors*[1] on behalf of one of the four appellant women, that the virtual courtroom was brimming with specialist silks, senior juniors, juniors, solicitors, and legal executives all focused on doing their best for the appellants, respondents and interveners they represented. We had assembled to argue about how the family courts should approach allegations of abuse and coercive control. We were about to appear before a mighty line-up of judges including the President of the Family Division. The wealth, breadth and depth of legal expertise deployed was extraordinary.

Yet, day in, day out, these cases are dealt with by those who have to operate on the frontline of the family justice system, whether they be high street solicitors, the junior Bar, lay justices, district judges or deputy district judges. We made the point in our submissions in *Re T* that the Court of Appeal could not take comfort in the small number of appeals that get to be argued before them, for these cases are the 'Cinderella' of the family justice system. Too many respondents are unrepresented. Lawyers' rates for those who are eligible for legal aid are so derisory that they are done for principle rather than profit. Too few decisions see the light of day in terms of appeal when mistakes are made. The sheer volume of cases involving domestic abuse suffocates the significance and complexity of the allegations involved. Would you have the experience or skill to act in a Crown Court on a charge involving anal rape? Would you defend on a charge of attempted strangulation? Would magistrates be considered the right forum to hear a case that in the criminal jurisdiction could carry a heavy sentence of imprisonment?

If we are to deliver justice to the families that come to us for advice and representation at the most stressful time of their lives then we need to treat this area of work with the seriousness it deserves. It's factually

---

1 [2021] EWCA Civ 448

complex, emotionally fraught and legally challenging. That is why this book is necessary.

It won't do the thinking for you; that's your responsibility. Read, research, do your homework. What you will find within its covers is an easy to follow, informative, practical guide that should prompt you to think and plan how to go about constructing and presenting your case. You should devour it. You should dig deeper into legal research and case law to ponder and answer for yourself some of the issues it throws up. Most of all, it should show you the value of proactive preparation – of the evidence, of the client, of the legal issues – because you need to be ready to argue points that could fundamentally change the way the trial is conducted and how it ends.

For us it may be a day in court for we have lives beyond the courtroom and litigation. For our clients, and the children at the heart of our family justice system, it can be a life-changing event for good or ill. Make their experience the best it can be in distressing circumstances. This book gives you the platform to build up your knowledge and experience. Use it. Expand upon it. Your clients deserve nothing less.

Professor Jo Delahunty QC
October 2021

PREFACE

"Domestic abuse in all its many forms, and whether directed at women, at men, or at children, continues, more than forty years after the enactment of the Domestic Violence and Matrimonial Proceedings Act 1976, to be a scourge on our society. Judges and everyone else in the family system need to be alert to the problems and appropriately focused on the available remedies. PD12J plays a vital part."[2]

This book is intended to be an 'every-day guide' for family law practitioners (particularly those at the start of their careers) on the treatment of domestic abuse allegations in private law children proceedings. We hope that litigants-in-person, and more widely, those interested in the inner workings of the family justice system, will find this text useful as well.

Some of the contents of this book may well be very familiar to experienced family lawyers. However, in our experience, the application of Practice Direction 12J can be patchy and inconsistent, and the pressures on the system as a whole can result in allegations of domestic abuse not being managed appropriately. We hope to equip practitioners with the tools they need to ensure that allegations of domestic abuse are dealt with robustly, fairly and sensitively in cases which concern disputes between parents about the upbringing of their children.

This is a fast-evolving area of law and all best endeavours have been made to ensure this book is accurate as at 28th October 2021.

Rebecca Cross
Malvika Jaganmohan
October 2021

---

[2] Sir J. Munby, '*President of Family Division circular: Practice Direction PD12J – Domestic Abuse*', 14th September 2017, accessed at familylawweek.co.uk

CONTENTS

Introduction		1
Chapter One	What Is Domestic Abuse?	11
Chapter Two	The Evolution of Practice Direction 12J	21
Chapter Three	Making the Application	33
Chapter Four	The First Hearing Dispute Resolution Appointment	45
Chapter Five	The Fact-Finding Hearing	71
Chapter Six	The Dispute Resolution Appointment (DRA)	97
Conclusion		109

INTRODUCTION

Domestic abuse is a common feature of many private law children practitioners' caseloads. In the year 2019/2020, the Family Court received 55,253 private law applications, of which it is thought at least 40% involve allegations of domestic abuse.[1] Joint research by Cafcass and Women's Aid found that in an (admittedly small) sample of 216 child contact cases, domestic abuse was alleged in 62% of cases, with fathers more likely to be the subject of allegations than mothers.[2] These statistics are perhaps unsurprising given that 'run of the mill' child contact disputes between parents would not necessarily need the intervention of the Family Court, with parents being able to agree contact arrangements amicably between themselves, perhaps with the assistance of mediation. We would, therefore, expect that victims and perpetrators of domestic abuse are over-represented in the family justice system.

The onset of the Covid-19 pandemic has only exacerbated the problem. Lockdown has left victims of domestic abuse even more isolated and vulnerable, with Women's Aid warning at the outset that *"social distancing and self-isolation will be used as a tool of coercive and controlling behaviour by perpetrators, and will shut down routes to safety and support."*[3] Between April and June 2020, there was a 65% increase in calls to the National Domestic Abuse Helpline, in comparison to the first three months of 2020.[4]

The treatment of domestic abuse allegations in the Family Court has come under increased scrutiny in recent years. Within a context of a greater push for transparency within the Family Court, the manner in

---

[1] *Re H-N & ors* [2021] EWCA Civ 448, at para. 3

[2] Cafcass and Women's Aid, '*Allegations of domestic abuse in child contact cases*', July 2017, accessed at cafcass.gov.uk

[3] Women's Aid, '*The impact of Covid-19 on women and children experiencing domestic abuse, and the life-saving services that support them*', 17th March 2020, accessed at womensaid.org.uk

[4] T. Havard, '*Domestic Abuse and Covid-19: A year into the pandemic*', 11th May 2021, accessed at commonslibrary.parliament.uk

which lawyers and judges deal with allegations of domestic abuse is under the spotlight.

Critical press coverage has painted the Family Court as out-of-date and out-of-touch, operating free from accountability and under a shroud of secrecy. In 2020, a circuit judge faced backlash following the scathing High Court judgment of Russell J in *JH v MF*,[5] in which she concluded that he had employed *"obsolescent concepts concerning the issue of consent."*[6] One headline read '*Female judge criticises male colleague who told woman she wasn't raped as she didn't fight back*'[7] while another headline to an article authored by a family law barrister herself declared: '*The courts' outdated views on domestic violence are putting vulnerable children at risk of harm*'.[8] A BBC news article reported that at least four children have been killed by a parent in the past five years after the Family Court granted contact.[9]

These headlines are just the tip of the iceberg. Journalist Louise Tickle has long reported on the goings-on of the Family Court. Recently, she sparked controversy with her Channel 4 Dispatches documentary '*Torn Apart: Family Courts Uncovered*'.[10] The documentary makes for uncomfortable viewing and features personal testimonies from a number of individuals who have had traumatic experiences of the family justice system. Tickle spends some time exploring the experiences of victims of domestic abuse within the system; Claire Waxman, Victims' Commissioner of London, says in the documentary that she hears from victims and survivors regularly *"just how re-victimising the process is"*. The

---

[5] [2020] EWHC 86 (Fam)

[6] ibid., at para. 54

[7] G. Swerling, '*Female judge criticises male colleague who told woman she wasn't raped as she didn't fight back*', The Telegraph, 22nd January 2020, accessed at telegraph.co.uk

[8] C. Proudman, '*The courts' outdated views on domestic violence are putting vulnerable children at risk of harm*', The Independent, 25th January 2020, accessed at independent.co.uk

[9] E. Ailes and J. Furst, '*Call for inquiry into abusive parents' access to children*', 15th May 2019, accessed at bbc.co.uk

[10] L. Tickle, '*Torn Apart: Family Courts Uncovered: Dispatches*', Channel 4, 2021, accessed at channel4.com

authors of this book are not taking a view on the observations in the documentary or the conclusions drawn, however it is important to note that the programme prompted both generous praise and vociferous criticism. This is indicative of just how polarising this subject is.

The treatment of domestic abuse by the Family Court is an understandably emotive topic. For the general public, it seems beyond belief that perpetrators of domestic abuse can retain parental rights and responsibilities. However, as lawyers, we are fully aware that the reality on the ground is far more nuanced than that. The Family Court finds itself between a rock and a hard place: on one hand, s1(2A) of the Children Act 1989 sets out the presumption that the involvement of a parent in a child's life will further the child's welfare (this is a controversial provision and it falls beyond the scope of this book to consider whether reform of s1(2A) is required). On the other hand, the Family Court needs to safeguard the parent who suffered the domestic abuse and the child from the harmful effects of that abuse.

In recent years, the courts and practitioners have developed a more sophisticated understanding of the impact of domestically abusive relationships on children. The new Domestic Abuse Act 2021 now codifies this in statute by specifying that any reference in the Act to a victim of domestic abuse includes a reference to a child who sees or hears, or experiences the effects of, the abuse.[11] This makes clear that domestic abuse and the child's welfare cannot be compartmentalised; domestic abuse forms part and parcel of the wider canvas of what is in the child's best interests. The Court of Appeal in *Re H-N & ors* endorsed this approach, observing that:

> *"A pattern of abusive behaviour is as relevant to the child as to the adult victim. The child can be harmed in any one or a combination of ways for example where the abusive behaviour:*
>
> i) *Is directed against, or witnessed by, the child;*

---

[11] s3(2)(a), Domestic Abuse Act 2021

ii) *Causes the victim of the abuse to be so frightened of provoking an outburst or reaction from the perpetrator that she/he is unable to give priority to the needs of her/his child;*

iii) *Creates an atmosphere of fear and anxiety in the home which is inimical to the welfare of the child;*

iv) *Risks inculcating, particularly in boys, a set of values which involve treating women as being inferior to men."*[12]

The Family Court must grapple with another tension: wanting to support victims of domestic abuse and safeguard them from re-traumatisation during the court proceedings on one hand; on the other hand, needing to robustly test allegations to determine where the truth lies before making orders that will have an enormous impact on a child's life and determine the trajectory of their relationship with the other parent.

Over the past eighteen months, the legal world has been exploring these issues through various initiatives. In March 2020, the President of the Family Division's Private Law Working Group produced their second interim report (the first having been published in July 2019) entitled *'Private law: family disputes – the time for change, the need for change, the case for change'*[13]. In this, they made clear that:

> "when considering the issue of domestic abuse, it is necessary to distinguish between short term heightened conflict which is a common feature of separation but is not necessarily or always harmful; persistent/chronic, unresolved conflict which is much more likely to result in emotional harm for the child with long-term consequences, and which will need to be taken into account when making a plan for

---

[12] *Re H-N & ors,* op. cit., at para. 31

[13] President of the Family Division's Private Law Working Group, *Private law: family disputes – the time for change, the need for change, the case for change'*, March 2020, accessed at judiciary.uk

child arrangements; and domestic abuse (in all its forms) which is undoubtedly harmful."[14]

That is, of course, easier said than done.

In June 2020, the *'Assessing Risk of Harm to Children and Parents in Private Law Children Cases'* ('the Harm Report'), was published by the Ministry of Justice. The aim of the report was to consider how effectively the Family Court deals with allegations of domestic abuse or other serious offences in private law children proceedings. The panel concluded that whilst it had:

"identified some good practice and widespread good intentions from those working under increasing pressure within the family justice system, it has also unveiled deep-seated and systematic issues that were found to affect how risk to both children and adults is identified and managed."[15]

In particular, the Harm Report identified four overarching barriers to the Family Court's ability to respond effectively to domestic abuse: the so-called "pro-contact" culture; the adversarial system; resource limitations; and silo working which inhibits coordination between courts and other organisations.[16] The Harm Report also recommended an urgent review of the presumption of parental involvement as set out in s1(2A) of the Children Act 1989.[17]

In March 2021, the judgment in the long-awaited conjoined domestic abuse appeals in *Re H-N & ors* was handed down by the Court of Appeal. Each of the four appeals was brought by mothers who were challenging the manner in which the court had dealt with their allegations of domestic abuse against the respondent fathers. While three of the appeals were allowed and important guidance was provided by the court about

---

[14] ibid., p17

[15] Ministry of Justice, *Assessing Risk of Harm to Children and Parents in Private Law Children Cases*, June 2020, at para. 7, accessed at gov.uk

[16] ibid., at p171

[17] ibid., at p175

the approach to be taken when there are such allegations in a private law children case, arguably the judgment did not say anything new or controversial. It confirmed that Practice Direction 12J ('PD12J'), the existing framework within which allegations of domestic abuse are considered in the Family Court, remains fit for purpose. The Court of Appeal appeared to be managing readers' expectations at the outset of the judgment, warning that:

> *"there is a limit to the extent to which we can give general guidance. In part, this is because there are various initiatives already in train... But it is also because there is plainly and properly a limit to what a constitution of the Court of Appeal, determining four individual appeals, can, and as a matter of law should, say about issues which do not strictly arise in any of those appeals."*[18]

It was perhaps unsurprising therefore that the judgment was considered by many organisations to be a missed opportunity to effect cultural change in the Family Court. Olive Craig of Rights of Women (one of the interveners in that case) wrote for *The Transparency Project*'s blog:

> *"What is so disappointing in the Court of Appeal's judgment is the failure to acknowledge how damning the Harm Panel Report is of the family justice system's response to parents who allege domestic abuse. The conclusion was that the family court is placing those parents and children at risk of harm from domestic abuse. The system which is meant to place children's welfare at its heart as its 'paramount consideration' is currently placing children at risk of domestic abuse. It is a scandal. Instead, in the paragraph immediately after the quote about coercive control above, the Court of Appeal went on to state:*
>
>> *'We are confident that the modern approach that we have described is already well understood and has become embedded through training and experience in the practice of the vast majority of judges and magistrates sitting in the Family Court.'*
>
> *"The Court's confidence in the face of the findings by the Harm Panel Report could only kindly be described as disappointing. What is clear*

---

[18] *Re H-N & ors,* op. cit., at para. 2

from the report and the evidence in the appeal cases, is that the approach described is not at all well understood. It is notable that the judgment refers to the training for all judges in issues around domestic abuse as grounds for confidence. The family court experiences of the women we speak to daily suggests to us that this training is not sufficient and the Court of Appeal's over-confidence in such training as a solution to the problems identified in the Harm Panel Report is an error."[19]

It falls outside the scope of this book to explore whether this is true and indeed, whether the Court of Appeal should have gone further.

The final development of interest that we will touch upon at this stage is the introduction of the Domestic Abuse Act 2021. This received Royal Assent on 29th April 2021, though not all sections of the Act are yet in force at the time of writing.[20] The scope of the Act is significant and includes a new statutory definition of domestic abuse. Notably, the definition includes coercive and controlling behaviour, economic abuse, psychological, emotional and other abuse[21], and as we have already discussed, the Act makes clear that a child who witnesses domestic abuse falls within the meaning of a 'victim' of domestic abuse.[22]

Victoria Atkins MP stated in respect of the Domestic Abuse Bill:

"We of course recognise the harm that is suffered by victims of domestic abuse. That is why the aim of the Bill is specifically to target it and raise awareness and understanding of its impact. It seeks to raise the profile of domestic abuse in all its forms, particularly given its pernicious nature, and to improve the effectiveness of the justice system in providing protection for victims and bringing perpetrators to justice. It also seeks to strengthen the support for victims and survivors provided by statutory agencies. The definition should help further in clarifying

---

[19] O. Craig, *'The Domestic Abuse appeals – a missed opportunity for cultural change?'*, The Transparency Project, accessed at transparencyproject.org.uk

[20] Domestic Abuse Act 2021 commencement schedule, accessed at gov.uk

[21] s1(3), Domestic Abuse Act 2021

[22] s3, Domestic Abuse Act 2021

the wide-ranging nature of domestic abuse for all those involved in the criminal justice system, at every level."[23]

Whether the Act has its desired effect remains to be seen but in the context of this hive of legal activity, this book is timely. The authors of this book are fully aware that the legal landscape is continually evolving, even as we write this. No doubt, in the coming months and years, more case law and analysis will emerge which will continue to impact our treatment of domestic abuse in the Family Court. However, we hope this guide is a helpful starting point for practitioners.

It is also important to note that the family justice system's ability to deal adequately with domestic abuse allegations relies on the system being properly resourced, which it simply is not. The system is on its knees. We need to recruit more judges to tackle the enormous backlog of court work. Those judges need to be appropriately trained, and not struggling with overwork and burnout. We need advocates who are not simply firefighting cases because of the huge pressure of work, but who are able to devote the attention to each case that their clients deserve. We need a properly funded legal aid system and we need to challenge the false economy which underpinned the devastating public funding cuts brought about by the Legal Aid, Sentencing and Punishment of Offenders Act 2012. Instead of the massive rise in litigants-in-person we have seen in recent years, we need parties who have the benefit of experienced legal representation so that cases are not unduly prolonged. The system is creaking and it has been for a very long time. Structural change is needed which will require the collective action of the entire profession to put pressure on those in power.

Let us make clear what this book is *not*. This book is not intended to comment on proposals for reform and it will not take a normative approach to the law. Although we are very much tempted, our intention is not to explore how the law *should* be, but how the law *is*, and how practitioners can make sure that they deal appropriately with allegations of domestic abuse within the existing framework.

---

[23] Domestic Abuse Bill Deb (Twelfth sitting), 17th June 2020, at col. 471, accessed at hansard.parliament.uk

This book is also not a 'how-to' guide on making applications for orders under the Children Act 1989. Our intention is to take readers through the process from start to finish, from the First Hearing Dispute Resolution Appointment ('FHDRA') to the Dispute Resolution Appointment ('DRA'), but focussing specifically on what practitioners should bear in mind when domestic abuse is an issue in a case. PD12J provides a comprehensive framework for dealing with allegations of domestic abuse however, as we will explore in Chapter Two, the challenge appears to have always been with its implementation rather than its contents.

Undoubtedly, this guide will not be exhaustive. However, our hope is that practitioners will be able to refer to this text at the beginning of a case or at court and think ahead about the issues which may arise and how they might go about addressing them.

Chapter One will consider the definition of domestic abuse and how it has evolved over time to encompass more broad-ranging types of abuse beyond physical violence.

Chapter Two will look at the evolution of PD12J since it appeared in its original form in 2008, and how it has developed in response to concerns that it is not having its desired effect.

Chapter Three will consider the C100 application form and what practitioners ought to bear in mind at the very beginning of a case when domestic abuse is an issue.

Chapters Four, Five and Six will look at the three key hearings in private law children matters – the FHDRA, the fact-finding hearing and the DRA – and how to make the most of these hearings to ensure appropriate outcomes for clients when there are allegations of domestic abuse to be resolved.

The concluding chapter will consider what changes are on the horizon; whether the Domestic Abuse Act 2021 and the decision in *Re H-N & ors* mark a sea-change in the Family Court's treatment of domestic abuse or whether they are simply more of the same; and what the system needs long-term to be able to deal with domestic abuse fairly and properly.

This is an emotive area of the law but, as lawyers, it is incumbent on us to be dispassionate when advising our clients. That does not mean that we should be unsympathetic to those who may have suffered domestic abuse, in its many forms. That does not mean that we should avoid interrogating the myths and assumptions which underpin decisions made by the Family Court concerning domestic abuse. However, whatever we might think of the state of the system and its shortcomings, it is a system within which we must work fearlessly in the best interests of our clients, and that is what we hope to assist other lawyers to do with this book.

A final remark: throughout this book, we will consider the impact of Covid-19 and remote hearings on our practices. At the time of writing, it has been over 18 months since the first UK lockdown was announced on 23rd March 2020. However, remote hearings still form a key feature of most family lawyers' day-to-day working lives. Even as we transition back to face-to-face hearings, it is likely that there will be a permanent place for remote hearings moving forward and so it is imperative that we consider how this will impact upon our approach to domestic abuse in private law children cases. Our clients must not feel that they are being afforded second-rate justice via a video link, with a distant, pixelated image dictating their lives and the lives of their children.

CHAPTER ONE

WHAT IS DOMESTIC ABUSE?

Societal understandings of what constitutes domestic abuse have evolved over time and, no doubt, will continue to evolve. Similarly, the Family Court's understanding of domestic abuse and its impact on children has also moved forward.

The Court of Appeal in *Re H-N & ors* tracked some of these developments in its wide-ranging judgment. It noted that the Domestic Violence and Matrimonial Homes Act 1976 introduced the concept of 'domestic violence' which, *"although ground breaking in its time, it is now wholly outdated and hard to comprehend an approach which required evidence of actual bodily harm to a victim before a power of arrest could be attached to an injunction..."*[24] The Court of Appeal also observed that *"[o]bsolete too is the approach often seen in the 1980s where... judges regarded that violence is purely a matter as between the adults and not as a factor that would ordinarily be relevant to determining questions about the welfare of their children."*[25]

The landmark 2001 Court of Appeal case of *Re L & ors (children)*[26] marked a sea-change in the Family Court's approach to private law children disputes where domestic abuse features. Its *"central conclusion... was that there needed to be a heightened awareness of the existence of, and the consequences for children of, exposure to 'domestic violence' between parents and other partners."*[27] The Court of Appeal considered the Children Act Sub-Committee of the Advisory Board on Family Law's report on parental contact in domestic violence cases, which made clear that where the issue of domestic violence is raised as a reason for limiting or refusing contact, the court should address the allegations at the earliest

---

[24] *Re H-N & ors*, op. cit., at para. 23

[25] ibid., at para. 24

[26] [2000] EWCA Civ 194

[27] *Re H-N & ors*, op. cit., at para. 24

opportunity, make findings of fact and decide on the effect of those findings on the question of contact. The court declined to conclude that there should be a presumption *against* contact where domestic violence has been alleged or proved. The court noted that, as a matter of principle, domestic violence in and of itself cannot constitute a bar to contact.

From reading the judgment, it is clear that the prevailing terminology at the time that *Re L & ors* was decided was 'domestic *violence*'. 'Domestic abuse' is the phrase now considered to be more appropriate, encompassing abuse in all its forms rather than focusing on simply physical violence.

Re L & ors pre-dated Practice Direction 12J ('PD12J'), the framework used by the Family Court when dealing with allegations of domestic abuse in private law children matters. PD12J was initially implemented in 2008 and has twice been updated; once in 2014 and again in 2017. The evolution of PD12J and what prompted its creation will be explored more fully in the next chapter.

The 2014 alteration substantially revised the definition of domestic violence as follows:

> *"**domestic violence**" means any incident or pattern of incidents of controlling, coercive or threatening behaviour, violence or abuse between those aged 16 or over who are or have been intimate partners or family members regardless of gender or sexuality. This can encompass, but is not limited to, psychological, physical, sexual, financial, or emotional abuse.*
>
> *"**controlling behaviour**" means an act or pattern of acts designed to make a person subordinate and/or dependent by isolating them from sources of support, exploiting their resources and capacities for personal gain, depriving them of the means needed for independence, resistance and escape and regulating their everyday behaviour.*
>
> *"**coercive behaviour**" means an act or a pattern of acts of assault, threats, humiliation and intimidation or other abuse that is used to harm, punish, or frighten the victim.*

"harm" means ill-treatment or the impairment of health or development including, for example, impairment suffered from seeing or hearing the ill- treatment of another; 'development' means physical, intellectual, emotional, social or behavioural development; 'health' means physical or mental health; and 'ill-treatment' includes sexual abuse and forms of ill-treatment which are not physical.

In 2017, the terminology was changed from domestic 'violence' to 'abuse' with its definition widened to include culturally specific forms of abuse, including spousal abandonment abroad.[28] In all other respects, the 2017 alteration retained the wording from the previous definition of 'domestic violence'.

There remains a terminology discrepancy within the Family Procedure Rules 2010 ('FPR 2010'). Both FPR 2010, r. 3.8 and its supporting practice direction, PD3A, refer to 'domestic violence' rather than 'domestic abuse'. This is indicative of a wider difficulty which is endemic amongst those working within the private family law arena, with the phrase 'domestic violence' often incorrectly being deployed by practitioners and judges alike. While this may seem to be nit-picking, language very much matters. For those working in the family justice system to show the general public and their clients that they have a sophisticated understanding of abuse in all its forms, it is important that we get the basics right. The phrase 'domestic abuse' more accurately reflects the full range of abuse, its complexities and the ongoing effects of the abuse post-separation on both the victim and the child.

Definitions

Practice Direction 12J

PD12J provides the following definition for domestic abuse:

"domestic abuse" includes any incident or pattern of incidents of controlling, coercive or threatening behaviour, violence or abuse between those aged 16 or over who are or have been intimate partners

---

[28] Practice Direction 12J, Family Procedure Rules 2010, at para. 3, accessed at justice.gov.uk

or family members regardless of gender or sexuality. This can encompass, but is not limited to, psychological, physical, sexual, financial, or emotional abuse. Domestic abuse also includes culturally specific forms of abuse including, but not limited to, forced marriage, honour-based violence, dowry-related abuse and transnational marriage abandonment.

Coercive and controlling behaviour is defined less broadly within PD12J:

*"**coercive behaviour**" means an act or a pattern of acts of assault, threats, humiliation and intimidation or other abuse that is used to harm, punish, or frighten the victim;*

*"**controlling behaviour**" means an act or pattern of acts designed to make a person subordinate and/or dependent by isolating them from sources of support, exploiting their resources and capacities for personal gain, depriving them of the means needed for independence, resistance and escape and regulating their everyday behaviour.*

In the 2021 High Court decision of *F v M*[29], Hayden J attempted to unpick the definitions of 'coercive behaviour' and 'controlling behaviour' in light of the difficulties identifying and evaluating the actions which amount to coercive and controlling behaviour. Hayden J observed that whilst individual acts relied upon may appear innocuous, it is only when those acts are considered against the backdrop of all the evidence that they bear a greater and more troubling significance. Hayden J also identified the potentially misleading definition within PD12J which suggests that a single incident of coercive or controlling behaviour may constitute domestic abuse, when *"behaviour… requires, logically and by definition, more than a single act."*[30] Hayden J repeats the following theme throughout his judgment:

"Key to assessing abuse in the context of coercive control is recognising that the significance of individual acts may only be understood properly within the context of wider behaviour. I emphasise it is the behaviour

---

[29] [2021] EWFC 4 (Fam)

[30] ibid., at para. 109

and not simply the repetition of individual acts which reveals the real objectives of the perpetrator and thus the true nature of the abuse."[31]

Hayden J breaks down the PD12J definition of coercive and controlling behaviour as follows[32]:

Coercive Behaviour:

- *a pattern of acts;*

- *such acts will be characterised by assault, threats, humiliation and intimidation but are not confined to this and may appear in other guises;*

- *the objective of these acts is to harm, punish or frighten the victim.*

Controlling Behaviour:

- *a pattern of acts;*

- *designed to make a person subordinate and/or dependent;*

- *achieved by isolating them from support, exploiting their resources and capacities for personal gain, depriving them of their means of independence, resistance and escape and regulating their everyday activities.*

Children Act 1989

Section 31(9) of the Children Act 1989 provides the following definitions:

---

[31] ibid.

[32] ibid., at para. 108

- 'Harm' means ill-treatment or damage to health and development, including, for example, damage suffered from seeing or hearing the ill-treatment of another.

- 'Health' means physical or mental health.

- 'Development' means physical, intellectual, emotional, social or behavioural development.

- 'Ill-treatment' includes sexual abuse and forms of ill-treatment which are not physical.

Whilst we acknowledge that section 31 is concerned with the making of public law orders rather than private law orders and the statutory definitions proffered are stated only to apply to that particular section, the same definitions are repeated on the first page of the C1A supplementary information court form, the form used to raise allegations of domestic abuse in a private law application.

Domestic Abuse Act 2021

The Domestic Abuse Act 2021 received Royal Assent on 29th April 2021. It provides a new definition of domestic abuse that applies to abusive behaviour between two people aged 16 or over who are personally connected to each other.

Section 1(3) contains the key definition:

Behaviour is 'abusive' if it consists of any of the following –

(a) physical or sexual abuse;

(b) violent or threatening behaviour;

(c) controlling or coercive behaviour;

(d) economic abuse (see subsection (4));

(e) psychological, emotional or other abuse;

and it does not matter whether the behaviour consists of a single incident or a course of conduct.

1(4) 'Economic abuse' means any behaviour that has a substantial adverse effect on B's ability to –

(a) acquire, use or maintain money or other property, or

(b) obtain goods or services.

Victims of domestic abuse can include children who are present.[33] Section 3 of the Domestic Abuse Act 2021 recognises that domestic abuse can impact on a child who sees or hears, or experiences the effects of the abuse and it treats such children as victims of domestic abuse in their own right where they are related to either the abuser or the abused.

Sections 1 to 2 of the Domestic Abuse Act 2021 came into force on 1st October 2021[34], while section 3 is due to come into force in Winter 2022.[35] However, in *Re H-N & ors* the Court of Appeal acknowledged that whilst the structure of the definition in the new Act is different to that within PD12J, the content is substantially the same.[36]

Final observations

In *Re H-N & ors* the Court of Appeal endorsed[37] the comments of Jackson LJ in *Re L (Relocation: Second Appeal)*[38]:

"Few relationships lack instances of bad behaviour on the part of one or both parties at some time and it is a rare family case that does not

---

[33] s1(5), Domestic Abuse Act 2021

[34] Pursuant to The Domestic Abuse Act 2021 (Commencement No. 2) Regulations 2021

[35] Domestic Abuse Act 2021 commencement schedule, accessed at gov.uk

[36] *Re H-N & ors*, op. cit., at para. 27

[37] ibid., at para. 32

[38] [2017] EWCA Civ 2121, at para. 61

> *contain complaints by one party against the other, and often complaints are made by both. Yet not all such behaviour will amount to 'domestic abuse', where 'coercive behaviour' is defined as behaviour that is 'used to harm, punish, or frighten the victim...' and 'controlling behaviour' as behaviour 'designed to make a person subordinate...' In cases where the alleged behaviour does not have this character it is likely to be unnecessary and disproportionate for detailed findings of fact to be made about the complaints; indeed, in such cases it will not be in the interests of the child or of justice for the court to allow itself to become another battleground for adult conflict."*

In short: previous poor behaviour between parents which is relied upon by a party to the proceedings must *directly concern the welfare of a child*. The Family Court does not entertain generalised mud-slinging. The onus is on practitioners to advise clients robustly about what is relevant and what is not; clients may well wish to throw 'everything and the kitchen sink' into the proceedings. To prevent fact-finding hearings from becoming unmanageably long (with the consequential delay to the proceedings and to the making of final decisions for children), careful thought needs to be given to what amounts to simply bad behaviour, and what amounts to domestic abuse. This can be a tricky line for practitioners to tread as, of course, we do not want clients to think us unsympathetic to their concerns.

Having said that, post-*Re H-N & ors*, we are likely to see an increasing reluctance by courts to prevent parties from raising allegations against the other party for fear of being appealed. Whilst *Re H-N & ors* reiterates the principle that case management lies with the tribunal, we suspect that many judges will be reluctant to closely examine whether something is or is not domestic abuse at an interim stage for fear of being appealed because they did not allow an alleged victim to put their case fully.

The Court of Appeal in *Re H-N & ors* also reminds practitioners that victims of domestic abuse do not have to be beyond reproach for the court to be able to make findings in their favour.[39] An individual does not have to be 'blameless' to be the victim of domestic abuse. As an

---

[39] *Re H-N & ors*, op. cit. at para. 218

example, the first-instance judge in one of the *Re H-N & ors* appeals presented the binary choice between:

> "*[a] relationship characterised by the deeply-controlling father described by the mother, a relationship in which she was blameless and under his spell? Or is the problem in this case the deeply-troubled mother with mental health difficulties unrelated to the father's behaviour and responsible herself for the wild, unboundaried behaviour described by the father.*"[40]

The Court of Appeal observed that while, of course, the credibility of the party alleging abuse is a live issue which requires careful assessment, a "*consideration of credibility will necessitate a wide consideration of all the circumstances*"[41] and the court should not encroach on the grounds of a psychiatric assessment "*with the focus turning both to the mother's mental stability and to her skills as a mother and a homemaker rather than whether she was the victim of domestic abuse*".[42]

Summary

The definition of domestic abuse has changed over time and it will continue to do so. No doubt, as practitioners, we still have much to learn about the insidious nature of domestic abuse and the many ways in which it can manifest.

The present definitions reinforce that non-physical abuse, with particular reference to coercive and controlling behaviour, can constitute domestic abuse. Indeed, the Court of Appeal in *Re H-N & ors* considered coercive and controlling behaviour to be "*central to the modern definitions of domestic abuse*"[43], noting that "*consideration of whether the evidence establishes an abusive pattern of coercive and/or controlling behaviour is likely to be the primary question in many cases where there is an allegation of*

---

[40] ibid., at para. 217

[41] ibid., at para. 219

[42] ibid., at para. 218

[43] ibid., at para. 29

domestic abuse, irrespective of whether there are other more specific factual allegations to be determined."[44]

We are pleased to see that a more sophisticated understanding of coercive and controlling behaviour is developing. Ongoing psychological and emotional abuse can build and systematically undermine the victim's personality and autonomy over many months or years, and can be just as harmful as black eyes and broken bones. However, coercive and controlling behaviour is a slippery concept which will require looking at the whole canvas of evidence. The practical difficulty with establishing coercive and controlling behaviour to the court's satisfaction remains and practitioners will need to grapple with this. The decision in *F v M* emphasises that context is everything.

---

[44] ibid., at para. 51

CHAPTER TWO

THE EVOLUTION OF PRACTICE DIRECTION 12J

The starting point for any practitioner when domestic abuse is an issue in a case is Practice Direction 12J ('PD12J').

PD12J is a 40-paragraph road-map for practitioners on how courts should approach allegations of domestic abuse in private law children cases. It is detailed and comprehensive. It is incumbent on lawyers and judges to make use of that framework.

It is worth noting that PD12J is a mandatory Practice Direction, not a discretionary one. It sets out what the Family Court or the High Court is *"required"* [45] to do in private law children cases where there are allegations of domestic abuse; not simply what it *may* do. Anecdotally, it is our experience that while many practitioners know in vague terms what PD12J says, often they do not know the detailed ins and outs of this wide-ranging Practice Direction. This means they are not able to hold the court to account when it fails to adhere to the requirements of PD12J.

There have been various iterations of PD12J over the years, which we touched upon in the previous chapter. The authors of this book consider it important to track the evolution of the Practice Direction so that practitioners can understand why certain changes came about and what they tell us about the gradual shift in attitudes towards the treatment of domestic abuse.

---

[45] Practice Direction 12J, op. cit., at para. 2

Practice Direction: Residence and Contact Orders: Domestic Violence and Harm

The first iteration of PD12J came in May 2008 from the then-President of the Family Division, Sir Mark Potter: '*Practice Direction: Residence and Contact Orders: Domestic Violence and Harm*'.

Cobb J suggests[46] that the Practice Direction was published originally in response to a report by Women's Aid entitled '*Twenty-nine child homicides: Lessons still to be learnt on domestic violence and child protection*'.[47] This harrowing report identified twenty-nine children from thirteen families who had been killed in a ten-year period by their fathers following parental separation. Eleven children in five cases were the subject of court proceedings.

Sir Nicholas Wall prepared a report[48] for the President of the Family Division in March 2006 in response to '*Twenty-nine child homicides…*' While he concluded that "*all the contact orders in the cases concerned were made in good faith and that the judges did their best conscientiously to apply section 1 of the Children Act 1989*"[49], and that he was satisfied that "*it would be wrong to hold any of the judges 'responsible' or 'accountable' for the deaths of any of the children, nor would it be appropriate for any form of disciplinary action to be instituted*"[50], he did, nevertheless, make a number of recommendations:

---

[46] Cobb J., '*Review of Practice Direction 12J FPR 2010 Child Arrangement and Contact Orders: Domestic Violence and Harm: Report to the President of the Family Division*', op. cit., at para. 7

[47] H. Saunders, '*Twenty-nine child homicides: Lessons still to be learnt on domestic violence and child protection*', Women's Aid, 2004, accessed at judiciary.uk

[48] N. Wall, '*A report to the President of the Family Division on the publication by the Women's Aid Federation of England entitled Twenty-nine child homicides: lessons still to be learnt on domestic violence and child protection with particular reference to the five cases in which there was judicial involvement*', March 2006, accessed at judiciary.uk

[49] ibid., at para. 8.7

[50] ibid., at para. 8.15

- The Family Justice Council be invited to consider and report to the President of the Family Division the approach to be taken by the courts to proposed consent orders in contact cases where domestic violence is in issue. He posed the question in his suggested terms of reference: "*When is it appropriate for a judge to refuse to approve a consent order agreed between well represented parents as to arrangements for their children, in circumstances when the court has not made any findings as to cross-allegations of domestic violence?*"[51] The Family Justice Council did subsequently prepare this report[52] and included amongst its recommendations the creation of a Practice Direction embodying the decision in *Re L & ors*, updated to reflect current best practice.

- In his preparation of the report, Sir Nicholas Wall was concerned to read in various places the proposition being advanced that it may be safe to direct contact when the violence has been directed towards the mother only.[53] He recommended reinforcing in a judgment or a lecture that it is a non-sequitur to consider that a father who has a history of violence towards the mother is, at the same time, a good father.[54]

- He strongly recommended that no judge sit for the first time in private law proceedings without having undergone multi-disciplinary training on domestic violence, as well as updating refresher courses.[55]

---

[51] ibid., at para. 8.27

[52] Family Justice Council, '*Report to the President of the Family Division on the approach to be adopted by the Court when asked to make a contact order by consent, where domestic abuse has been an issue in the case*', 2007, accessed at judiciary.uk

[53] ibid., at para. 8.22

[54] ibid., at para. 8.28

[55] ibid., at para. 8.29

The contents of the original Practice Direction may look familiar to practitioners and set out the key principles which underpin PD12J as we now know it, including that:

> *The court must, at all stages of the proceedings, consider whether domestic violence is raised as an issue, either by the parties or otherwise, and if so must:*
>
> - *identify at the earliest opportunity the factual and welfare issues involved;*
>
> - *consider the nature of any allegation or admission of domestic violence and the extent to which any domestic violence which is admitted, or which may be proved, would be relevant in deciding whether to make an order about residence or contact and, if so, in what terms;*
>
> - *give directions to enable the relevant factual and welfare issues to be determined expeditiously and fairly.*[56]

The Practice Direction was re-issued in January 2009 to reflect the decision of the House of Lords in *Re B (Children)*[57], namely the observations of Baroness Hale that:

> *"the finding of those facts is merely part of the whole process of trying the case. It is not a separate exercise. And once it is done the case is part heard. The trial should not resume before a different judge, any more than any other part heard case should do so. In the particular context of care proceedings, where the character and personalities of the parties are important components in any decision, it makes no sense at all for one judge to spend days listening to them give evidence on one issue and for another judge to send more days listening to them give evidence on another. This is not only a wasteful duplication of effort. Much useful information is likely to fall between the gaps. How can a judge who*

---

[56] *Practice Direction: Residence and Contact orders: Domestic Violence and Harm*, issued on 9th May 2008 and re-issued on 14th January 2009, at para. 3, accessed at judiciary.uk

[57] [2008] UKHL 35

has not heard the parents give their evidence about how the child's injuries occurred begin to assess the risk of letting them care for the child again? The experts may make their assessments, but in the end it is for the judge to make the decision on all the evidence before him. How can he properly do that when he has heard only half of it?"[58]

As such, paragraphs 15 and 23 of the re-issued Practice Direction set out that when the court fixes a fact-finding hearing, it must *at the same time* fix a further hearing for determination of the application. The hearings should be conducted by the same judge or, in the magistrates' court, by at least the same chairperson of the justices. Exceptions may be made where trying to secure judicial continuity would delay the timetable and the judge or chairperson is satisfied (and the reasons why must be recorded in writing) that the negative impact on the child's welfare would outweigh the negative impact to the fair trial of the proceedings.

We will return to this in Chapter Six as this element of PD12J frequently goes unobserved.

2014 revision

The first revision of PD12J came in 2014, following a 2013 report[59] by Professor Rosemary Hunter and Adrienne Barnett for the Family Justice Council which concluded that the Practice Direction "*is not operating as intended*" and that the "*problems with implementation are both cultural and material.*"[60] In that report, Hunter and Barnett presented the results of a national survey of judicial officers and practitioners on the implementation of the Practice Direction. They noted that many of the survey respondents "*appear to hold narrow, legalistic views of what constitutes domestic violence, of the effects of domestic violence and the harm resulting from it, and of the risk of future violence*"[61] and they also found

---

[58] ibid., at para. 76

[59] R. Hunter and A. Barnett, '*Fact-Finding Hearings and the Implementation of the President's Practice Direction: Residence and Contact Cases: Domestic Violence and Harm*', op. cit.

[60] ibid., at p8

[61] ibid., at p72

that implementation of PD12J *"is hampered by severe resource limitations"*[62] (a situation which has likely only worsened in recent years after devastating legal aid cuts and austerity measures).

Amongst its recommendations, the report suggested that there may be merit in revising the Practice Direction *"to expand the definition of domestic violence, appropriately incorporate the guidance on split hearings and clarify points that continue to be subject to varying interpretations."*[63]

Accordingly, the 2014 version of PD12J was amended to include a revised definition of domestic abuse that was far more broad-ranging and fit for the times. As helpfully summarised by Cobb J, the 2014 version also saw the inclusion of a statement of General Principles as a judicial aid to the application of the Practice Direction, the prescription of clearer expectations in relation to fact-finding hearings and tighter provisions for the making of interim child arrangement orders.[64]

2017 revision

Despite the attempts at tightening up PD12J in 2014, problems persisted. In 2016, the President of the Family Division commissioned a review[65] of PD12J by Cobb J (who had been chair of the Private Law Working Group when PD12J was revised in 2014). This review was prompted by a further troubling Women's Aid report in January 2016 entitled *'Nineteen Child Homicides: What must change so children are put first in child contact arrangements and the family courts'*[66], which covered a ten-year period in which nineteen children from twelve families were

---

[62] ibid., at p8

[63] ibid., at p73

[64] Cobb J., *'Review of Practice Direction 12J FPR 2010 Child Arrangement and Contact Orders: Domestic Violence and Harm: Report to the President of the Family Division'*, op. cit., at para. 7

[65] Cobb J., *'Review of Practice Direction 12J FPR 2010 Child Arrangement and Contact Orders: Domestic Violence and Harm'*, op. cit.

[66] Women's Aid, *'Nineteen Child Homicides: what must change so children are put first in child contact arrangements and the family courts'*, February 2016, accessed at womensaid.org.uk

killed by their fathers in circumstances relating to child contact (formally or informally arranged). One of the report's recommendations was that the Ministry of Justice must ensure that all family courts including judges and involved statutory agencies are aware of and fully implement PD12J[67], and that there is an urgent need for independent, national oversight into the implementation of PD12J.[68]

The Women's Aid report was followed by a parliamentary hearing convened by the All Party Parliamentary Group ('APPG') on Domestic Violence[69] and a parliamentary briefing paper.[70] The record of the parliamentary hearing makes for disturbing reading, while the briefing paper reported that implementation of the Practice Direction was "*patchy*", with "*variable awareness*" amongst the judiciary.[71]

Cobb J's recommended revisions to PD12J included the following:

- As previously discussed in this book, s1(2A) of the Children Act 1989 sets out that the court is to presume "*unless the contrary is shown, that involvement of that parent in the life of the child concerned will further the child's welfare*". Women's Aid and the APPG raised concerns that this effectively operates to require "*contact at all costs*" in all cases.[72] Cobb J recommended that where the involvement of a parent in a child's life would place the child or other parent at risk of suffering harm from abuse, the presumption be displaced.[73]

---

[67] ibid., at p25

[68] ibid., at p35

[69] Hansard Vol 614, Col 1081, accessed at hansard.parliament.uk

[70] APPG on Domestic Violence and Women's Aid, '*Domestic Abuse, Child Contact and the Family Courts: Parliamentary Briefing*', April 2016, accessed at womensaid.org.uk

[71] ibid., at p17

[72] ibid, at p12

[73] Cobb J., '*Review of Practice Direction 12J FPR 2010 Child Arrangement and Contact Orders: Domestic Violence and Harm*', op. cit., at para. 12(a).

- An explicit requirement in the Practice Direction that the court ensure that the court process is not used as a means to perpetuate coercion, control or harassment by an abusive parent.[74]

- A proposal for courts to consider more carefully the waiting arrangements at court prior to the hearing, and arrangements for entering and exiting the building.[75] The APPG and Women's Aid's briefing paper reported that it is not uncommon for women to be followed, stalked, harassed and further traumatised after leaving the court.[76]

- Enhanced protections for cross-examination of alleged victims of domestic abuse, to include a prohibition on unrepresented alleged abusers cross-examining the alleged victim.[77]

- Where domestic abuse has been proved, the court shall obtain a risk assessment conducted by a specialist domestic abuse practitioner working for an appropriately accredited agency. If the risk assessment concludes that a parent poses a risk to a child or to the other parent, supported contact in a contact centre or contact supervised by a parent or relative is not appropriate.[78]

- Greater consistency and clarity of language within the practice direction by adopting a common test of *"protection from risk of harm"*.[79]

---

[74] ibid., at para. 12(b).

[75] ibid., at para. 12(c). See also: Family Procedure Rules 2010, Practice Direction 12J, at para. 10.

[76] APPG on Domestic Violence and Women's Aid, *'Domestic Abuse, Child Contact and the Family Courts: Parliamentary Briefing'*, op. cit., at p16

[77] Cobb J., *'Review of Practice Direction 12J FPR 2010 Child Arrangement and Contact Orders: Domestic Violence and Harm'*, op. cit., at para. 12(d)

[78] ibid., at para. 12(e). See also: Practice Direction 12J, op cit., at paras. 33(a) and 38.

[79] ibid., at para. 12(f)

- Where there are disputed or undetermined allegations of domestic abuse, the court should not make an interim child arrangements order unless it is satisfied that the child and the parent who has made the allegation and is at any time caring for the child are not exposed to a risk of harm (bearing in mind the impact which domestic violence against a parent can have on the emotional well-being of the child, the safety of the parent, and the need to protect against controlling or coercive behaviour) and that the order is in the best interests of the children.[80]

The President of the Family Division at the time, Sir James Munby, largely accepted Cobb J's recommendations. Cobb J's proposed prohibition on alleged perpetrators of domestic abuse cross-examining alleged victims was not one of the recommendations adopted; the President's view was that this is a matter for primary legislation rather than a Practice Direction[81] and indeed, the Domestic Abuse Act 2021 now makes provision for this. We explore this in more detail in Chapter Five.

The draft amended PD12J was considered by the Family Justice Council and by the Family Procedure Rule Committee, and on 14th September 2017, the President issued a circular attaching the revised Practice Direction, which came into force on 2nd October 2017.

It should be noted that while Sir James Munby wrote that *"Subject only to one point [the proposed prohibition on alleged perpetrators of domestic abuse cross-examining alleged victims] I accept all [Cobb J's] recommendations and wish to see them implemented, in full and as soon as possible"*[82], it does not appear that *all* of Cobb J's other amendments to PD12J were in fact incorporated, or certainly not the precise wording that he proposed. For instance, his proposed amendment making clear that the court should ensure the court process is not being used as a means in itself to perpetuate coercion, control and harassment by an abusive

---

[80] ibid., at p17. See also: Practice Direction 12J, op. cit., at paras. 25 to 26.

[81] J. Munby, '*16th View from the President's Chambers: Children and vulnerable witnesses: where are we?*' [2017] Fam Law 151, p160-161

[82] ibid.

parent does not appear in PD12J in its present form. In addition, Cobb J's proposed amendment that where the involvement of a parent in a child's life would put the child or other parent at risk of suffering harm arising from domestic violence or abuse, the presumption in section 1(2A) of the Children Act 1989 shall not apply was also not incorporated in the form he suggested. Readers will note the more cautious wording in paragraph 7 of PD12J in respect of the statutory presumption in section 1(2A) of the Children Act 1989.

Summary

And so, we arrive at PD12J as we know it now. The authors of this book do not propose to set out PD12J in laborious detail in this chapter. Not only can practitioners access that quite easily for themselves, in our view it would be more productive to weave the relevant elements of PD12J into our analysis of the approach to be taken throughout the court proceedings in the chapters to follow.

However, before we do that, it is important to contextualise the Practice Direction. For more than thirteen years, there has been criticism levelled at PD12J for offering inadequate protection to victims of domestic abuse. It appears that this criticism has not so much been about the *contents* of the Practice Direction itself, but the *implementation* of the Practice Direction by judges and magistrates.

The Court of Appeal in *Re H-N & ors* concluded that:

> "*PD12J is and remains, fit for the purpose for which it was designed namely to provide the courts with a structure enabling the court first to recognise all forms of domestic abuse and thereafter on how to approach such allegations when made in private law proceedings. As was also recognised by The Harm Panel, we are satisfied that the structure properly reflects modern concepts and understanding of domestic abuse. The challenge relates to the proper implementation of PD12J.*"[83]

---

[83] op. cit., at para. 28

As we continue to grapple with the correct treatment of domestic abuse in the family courts, no doubt that challenge will remain. This book is an attempt to try and assist lawyers with tackling that challenge head-on, insofar as we are able.

Experienced lawyers reviewing this history of PD12J will sadly note that many of the critiques of the Practice Direction have been raised over and over again by various individuals and agencies, with little practical change to the reality on the ground. For all that lawyers can try to approach PD12J more robustly – and we hope this book assists them to do so – there is much that falls outside our control and which will require structural change: lack of judicial training; crowded court listings; a lack of judges and courtrooms; the unavailability of legal aid. Proper implementation of PD12J requires not only cultural change but a properly-resourced family justice system; but that is a subject for another day and another book.

CHAPTER THREE
MAKING THE APPLICATION

Applicants for orders under the Children Act 1989 who allege they are the victims of domestic abuse can take certain steps to ensure that this remains at the forefront of the court's analysis of risk from the outset, and to ensure that they are appropriately safeguarded during the court proceedings. This starts with the application form.

Claiming a MIAM exemption

In all private law disputes involving children, parties must attend a Mediation Information Assessment Meeting ('MIAM') before commencing an application with the court. There is no requirement to attend a MIAM where issues of domestic abuse are involved but a declaration as part of the C100 must be signed to confirm the exemption.

Where a MIAM exemption is claimed due to domestic abuse, the C100 form (the form used to apply for an order pursuant to section 8 of the Children Act 1989) requires the applicant to confirm that there is evidence of domestic abuse and to specify what that evidence is by reference to a list of twenty-one different forms of evidence. It would be sensible for the applicant to supply a copy of their 'evidence' to their solicitor/legal adviser immediately upon instructing them.

In cases where domestic abuse is alleged but the applicant does not have the required form of evidence for a MIAM exemption, there is another route by which they can secure the exemption. If they attend mediation, the mediator can exempt the applicant on the basis that *"mediation is otherwise not suitable as a means of resolving the dispute"*.[84] This provision acts somewhat as a safeguard for those who have not previously disclosed their domestic abuse or were unaware that their experiences constituted domestic abuse; something which occurs routinely. However, this

---

[84] Family Procedure Rules 2010, r. 3.8(2)(c)

safeguard is not a panacea; mediators may be insufficiently trained and unable to identify the signs of domestic abuse, particularly more 'slippery' forms of abuse such as coercive and controlling behaviour.

Section 80 of the Domestic Abuse Act 2021 prohibits relevant health professionals from charging a fee to provide "relevant evidence", that is:

- evidence that the individual is, or is at risk of being, a victim of domestic abuse which is intended to support an application by the individual for civil legal services, or

- any other evidence that the individual is, or is at risk of being, a victim of domestic abuse which is of a description specified in regulations made by the Secretary of State.

This provision came into force on 1st October 2021 and will, hopefully, put an end to the practice of general practitioners and hospitals charging fees to provide information which the applicant needs, for example, to obtain legal aid.

The C100

An application for any order pursuant to section 8 of the Children Act 1989 is commenced using the C100 form. Within the C100 the applicant must identify the reasons for bringing the application to the court and set out what they want the court to do.

The form is straightforward to complete. Some sections require narrative answers although the boxes for these answers are very small and it is quite usual for a continuation sheet to be used which will allow the party to provide more details. It would be wise to make use of the continuation sheet; this is the first opportunity the applicant has to provide a narrative with respect to the domestic abuse they are alleging and how they say it should influence the child arrangements. They should not feel that their ability to paint a full picture to the court of the abuse they have experienced is hindered by the format of the application form.

The C1A

Where a party is alleging that domestic abuse has been a feature of their relationship a C1A *'Allegations of harm and domestic violence (Supplemental information form)'* is to be completed alongside the C100. The other party has the opportunity, though it is not required, to respond to the allegations using the same form. Indeed, it is not unusual for the respondent to the application to be the first party to fill in a C1A if the applicant is the one seeking contact and the respondent is concerned that this would not be safe. Again, very limited space is given in the C1A and the use of a separate continuation sheet is recommended.

It is imperative that the C100 and the C1A are completed as fully and accurately as possible to enable Cafcass to complete their initial safeguarding enquiries and to enable the court to list the matter before the appropriate level of judge. Paragraph 9 of PD12J specifies:

> *Where any information provided to the court before the FHDRA[85] or other first hearing (whether as a result of initial safeguarding enquiries by Cafcass or CAFCASS Cymru or on form C1A or otherwise) indicates that there are issues of domestic abuse which may be relevant to the court's determination, the court must ensure that the issues are addressed at the hearing, and that the parties are not expected to engage in conciliation or other forms of dispute resolution which are not suitable and/or safe.*

The court would not be able to do this satisfactorily at the FHDRA without the parties fully appraising it of the issues in either the application form, the C1A or the safeguarding interview with Cafcass which takes place prior to the FHDRA (the latter is usually quite brief and parties often find themselves flustered and forget to mention important pieces of information in the heat of the moment).

Although, of course, every single incident of domestic abuse cannot be identified in any one document – particularly if the parties were in a long

---

[85] Short for 'First Hearing Dispute Resolution Appointment'. This is the first hearing in the proceedings (unless there has been an urgent hearing prior to this) and is discussed more fully in the next chapter.

relationship – the court should have a clear idea of what the most serious allegations are when they read the C100 and the C1A. It is not unusual for clients to face criticism further within the proceedings for raising serious allegations which were not mentioned at the outset in their application form. This may also prompt questions about their credibility and why the allegations are surfacing so late in the day.

The C1A often acts as the first draft of the Scott Schedule, that is, the schedule prepared by the person alleging domestic abuse in due course which sets out their allegations in tabular form. If prepared properly, the C1A can reduce work for practitioners further down the line when they are directed to prepare schedules or otherwise set out the client's allegations.

One bad habit that many practitioners and courts have fallen into is encouraging clients or parties to identify the "first, worst and last" incidents. We would urge against that approach. As *Re H-N & ors* made very clear, coercion and control is an overarching pattern of behaviour into which specific incidents of domestic abuse fit. Within this context, the "first, worst and last" strategy is demonstrably out of date.

Practitioners will be aware that Scott Schedules appear to be falling out of favour. The decision in *Re H-N & ors* noted that:

> "*[o]ne striking feature of the dozen oral submissions heard during the hearing of these appeals was that there was effective unanimity that the value of Scott Schedules in domestic abuse cases had declined to the extent that, in the view of some, they were a potential barrier to fairness and good process, rather than an aid.*"[86]

One of the criticisms levelled at Scott Schedules is that they artificially restrict parties from painting a nuanced picture of the abuse they have suffered by requiring them to identify individual incidents in a restrictive, tabular form rather than allowing them to present a pattern of behaviour. Nonetheless, until a suitable replacement for the Scott Schedule is identified, it is likely that some judges will continue to use them.

---

[86] *Re H-N & ors*, op. cit., at para. 43

The table of allegations in the C1A invites the parties to provide the following details:

- when the behaviour started and for how long it continued;

- the nature of the behaviour;

- whether help was sought, and if so, from whom;

- what help, if any, was provided by the person from whom help was requested (the person/organisation who provides the help may often be the same as the one who supports the mediation exemption, for example).

Whilst a date range for the behaviour is requested, the form does reassure the party that the start date does not need to be the exact date, and the party can indicate if the abuse is ongoing. The C1A also offers the party the option of providing a narrative summary addressing any other concerns about their child's safety and wellbeing. Those filling in this form should not feel pressured to only particularise clearly identifiable individual incidents because of the format of the C1A. If the headline allegation is coercive and controlling behaviour, this can be made clear in the C1A, perhaps with illustrative examples. The form is intended to be a guide rather than a restraint and no judge should criticise an applicant for failing to particularise individual incidents which do not fit neatly into the form's boxes, particularly if the applicant is alleging a pattern of behaviour.

The C1A invites the applicant to specify what steps or orders they want the court to take or make to protect them or their child. This section is somewhat misleading as the only examples the form gives, listed exhaustively, are a non-molestation order, a prohibited steps order or a specific issue order. Of course, the options are far broader than that (for example, an interim child arrangements order that the child lives with the applicant and have no/limited contact with the other parent).

There are tick-box questions where the applicant can indicate whether or not they agree to unsupervised, supervised or indirect contact. This is arguably unhelpful because it may be that the applicant does not yet know what they propose in terms of child arrangements; they may wish for there to be a fact-finding hearing or for the court to complete a risk assessment prior to settling their view on the child arrangements moving forward. Again, if the applicant feels uncomfortable 'pinning their colours to the mast' at this early stage, it may be advisable not to tick any of the prescribed boxes and simply to set out in writing in a convenient place that their view is not yet settled and they do not know. Otherwise, there is a risk that the applicant – under pressure to fill in the form – signs themselves up to child arrangements with which they are not entirely comfortable and which the respondent may later rely on in the court proceedings as evidence of their agreement.

What other orders might be needed?

In cases involving domestic abuse, it is common, though not necessary, for the applicant to apply for a prohibited steps order ('PSO') alongside a child arrangements order ('CAO'). A PSO prevents the respondent from doing something without the permission of the court or the applicant parent, such as removing the children from their school/nursery or from the applicant's care. This may be appropriate if, for example, the respondent parent has threatened to abduct the children from school. The court may make an interim PSO at the first hearing as a 'holding position', sometimes until the conclusion of the proceedings. This allows the court to keep the children safe whilst any risk is robustly assessed during the court process. Practitioners need to discuss this option with the client and determine at the outset whether a PSO is needed to protect the children in the interim.

Alongside applications under the Children Act 1989, applicants may also wish to consider seeking orders pursuant to Part IV of the Family Law Act 1996 if they feel particularly at risk (such as an occupation order to secure the family home or a non-molestation order to protect them from harm). The court, in due course, may wish to consolidate the two sets of proceedings to prevent duplication of analysis and to deal with matters in a more streamlined manner.

Is an urgent hearing or a without notice hearing required?

The C100 allows the applicant to seek an urgent hearing. It is imperative that this option is not misused because of the already over-stretched family justice system; a stressed and overworked judge will not be impressed by opportunistic applications for urgent orders.

The C100 requires the applicant to specify why an urgent hearing is required. If the applicant is the one alleging the domestic abuse, has separated from the respondent and has the child safely and securely in their care, it is unlikely an urgent hearing is required. The C100 sets out at section 3(c) tick-box examples of what might constitute urgency, for instance a risk of harm to a child or a risk of unlawful removal of a child from the United Kingdom.

A without notice hearing (that is, a hearing which takes place without the knowledge of the respondent) can also be sought via the C100. Again, this option should not be misused. The FL401 application form which is used by those seeking orders under Part IV of the Family Law Act 1996 helpfully sets out the circumstances in which a without notice order may be made (mirroring s45(2) of the Family Law Act 1996). The court will consider all the circumstances of the case, including:

- Any risk of significant harm to the applicant or a relevant child, attributable to conduct of the respondent, if the order is not made immediately;

- Whether it is likely that the applicant will be deterred or prevented from pursuing the application if an order is not made immediately;

- Whether there is reason to believe that the respondent is aware of the proceedings but is deliberately evading service and that the applicant or a relevant child will be seriously prejudiced by the delay involved.

Special measures

Section 7 of the C1A includes a list of proposed special measures which the applicant may wish to request to keep themselves safe and to be able to give their full and best evidence to the court. Those most relevant to cases involving domestic abuse are as follows:

- separate waiting rooms;

- separate exits and entrances;

- screens;

- video links;

- separate toilets;

- advance viewing of the Court.

However, these measures are not exhaustive. Rather than simply putting the possible options in the C1A to their clients, practitioners should consider asking the open question: "what do you need to feel safe in the courtroom?" This gives clients the space to think creatively around how they can be protected during the proceedings and to explore options which are not set out in the C1A form. For example, one problem that arises frequently is that the parties attend court at the same time for the listed hearing, which risks the alleged victim coming face-to-face with the alleged abuser. In the application form, the applicant could consider requesting that the court direct that the parties attend court at different times for the FHDRA to avoid the prospect of them coming into contact.

Unfortunately, practitioners are not unused to attending court (either virtually or in person) only to find that requested measures have not been made available, or that insufficient thought has been given to the participation of the alleged victim of domestic abuse. Legal representatives should chase the court ahead of each hearing to ensure that the requested special measures are in place. They may also wish to attend court earlier than the time they are required to be in attendance to see if any arrangements can be made, if they have not been already.

Special measures will be considered more fully in the next chapter.

Form C8

Form C8 is to be used by any party in family proceedings who does not wish to reveal their contact details to the other party. If this is applicable, their contact details are to be listed on this form and **not** on the C100 or the C1A. Contact details are required by the court for the purposes of liaising with the parties about hearings, sending correspondence to them, and enabling Cafcass to complete their safeguarding enquiries.

Eligibility for legal aid

Legal aid availability in private law children proceedings has been severely restricted by the implementation of the Legal Aid, Sentencing and Punishment of Offenders Act 2012. It is noteworthy that in *Re H-N & ors*[87], all the appellant mothers were eligible for public funding while all of the respondent fathers were represented by solicitors and counsel acting pro bono. The number of litigants-in-person in the family courts has risen enormously. Not only might this create an imbalance of power between the parties in their ability to present their cases effectively, for alleged victims of domestic abuse, it is troubling that there is no additional professional barrier between them and the unrepresented alleged abuser.

This book does not purport to analyse in any great detail the complex rules around legal aid eligibility in private law children disputes. However, broadly speaking, where the applicant is the victim of domestic abuse or the child has suffered domestic abuse, they may qualify for legal aid provided evidence is available of this, as prescribed in the Civil Legal Aid (Procedure) Regulations 2012. Again, this requirement to provide evidence is problematic because many victims of domestic abuse do not

---

[87] op. cit., at para. 16

report allegations of abuse, or they may not recognise at the time that they are suffering domestic abuse.

In order to qualify for legal aid, the applicant must also be of limited means. The Legal Aid Agency (LAA) defines this as an income (single or combined income if with a partner) of no more than £2,657 a month before tax, and savings of no more than £8,000. The limited means must be evidenced.

The Government website directs prospective applicants to local solicitors or 'legal advisers' for further advice with respect to the means criterion and the evidence in support which is required. Alternatively, the applicant can complete a lengthy online form which collates information regarding the applicant's relationship status, benefit income, property, savings (to include non-essential items worth over £500), income and tax and outgoings. The website states it can *only* provide the applicant with *guidance* on whether or not they will qualify for legal aid and again directs the applicant to a legal adviser. The full eligibility criteria are set out in the Civil Legal Aid (Financial Resources and Payment for Services) Regulations 2013.

Even if a party is not eligible for legal aid, they may be able to get assistance with paying the court fee by completing the Form EX160, which is available online.

Summary

This chapter does not set out exhaustively what applicants should bear in mind when applying for private law orders under the Children Act 1989. That is not the purpose of this book. However, what we have aimed to do is to encourage practitioners to think about what issues arise within the application process by virtue of domestic abuse being alleged.

Whilst an application often has to be issued at short notice in cases involving domestic abuse and applicants will not have the opportunity to spend days refining their application, it is still essential that the form is completed thoroughly and accurately and all concerns around domestic abuse, as far as they can be, are raised. Throughout proceedings the court will refer back to the initial application to ascertain what the applicant is seeking and why. As we have already said, the C100 and the C1A is the first opportunity the applicant has to shape the narrative.

Alongside making the application, the applicant should begin evidence-gathering (as far as they are able to in the absence of any court order directing that this information be shared by relevant agencies). Any documentary evidence alluded to in the C100 or in the C1A form will likely be directed at the FHDRA or later in proceedings.

Checklist for the application form

If issues of domestic abuse have been raised, have you considered the following?

- ☐ Is the client able to obtain an exemption from attending a MIAM?

- ☐ Have the allegations of domestic abuse/responses to the allegations been set out in sufficient detail in the C100 and the C1A forms?

- ☐ Does the client feel comfortable specifying in the C1A form whether they agree to unsupervised, supervised or indirect contact? Would they prefer to await any fact-finding hearing/risk assessment by the court before forming a view?

- ☐ What orders are needed to keep the client/the child safe in the interim?

- ☐ Is an urgent or without notice hearing required?

- ☐ Does the client require any special measures?

- ☐ Has the court been contacted ahead of the hearing to confirm that any requested special measures are in place?

- ☐ Has a Form C8 been completed if the client wishes to keep their contact details confidential?

☐ Is the client eligible for legal aid or assistance with paying the court fee? Are they able to provide evidence to the LAA that they have been the victim of domestic abuse?

CHAPTER FOUR

THE FIRST HEARING DISPUTE RESOLUTION APPOINTMENT

The First Hearing Dispute Resolution Appointment ('FHDRA') is a hearing that, too often, is dealt with in a haphazard manner which then sets the tone for the remainder of the proceedings. Despite the name, family justice practitioners will know that more often than we would like, very little happens by way of 'dispute resolution' at the FHDRA in cases which involve domestic abuse. The purpose of the FHDRA is either to narrow the issues in dispute between the parties or, if that cannot be done, to make directions to obtain the evidence needed by the court so that it has all the information it requires to make a determination on the disputed issues.

Since the onset of the Covid-19 pandemic, FHDRAs have become chaotic. There are various reasons for this, including:

- Delays in listing FHDRAs from the point of issuing proceedings because of a lack of judicial and courtroom availability.

- An unmanageable workload for Cafcass which frequently leads to delays in completion of safeguarding checks. In our experience, it is not unusual to turn up to a listed FHDRA only to be told that the safeguarding letter remains outstanding, very little can be accomplished, and an adjourned FHDRA will need to be listed.

- Many courts routinely listing FHDRAs before legal advisers sitting alone without a panel of lay justices. A legal adviser sitting alone can only endorse agreed orders; if the parties wish for the court to determine any disputed issue whatsoever, the legal adviser is powerless to do this.

- Communications between the court and other overstretched agencies have broken down leading to mishaps such as missing interpreters.

- FHDRAs generally take place via telephone or video link leading to the usual technological difficulties which have become characteristic of pandemic working.

- On occasion, no FHDRA takes place at all, with the court dealing with the matter on paper. This can mean that parties may not make it into a courtroom until the Dispute Resolution Appointment ('DRA'), many months into the proceedings.

So how *should* FHDRAs be dealt with and what does Practice Direction 12J ('PD12J') say about them?

Paragraph 5 of PD12J sets out that:

The court must, at all stages of the proceedings, and specifically at the First Hearing Dispute Resolution Appointment ('FHDRA'), consider whether domestic abuse is raised as an issue, either by the parties or by Cafcass or CAFCASS Cymru or otherwise, and if so must –

- *identify at the earliest opportunity (usually at the FHDRA) the factual and welfare issues involved;*

- *consider the nature of any allegation, admission or evidence of domestic abuse, and the extent to which it would be likely to be relevant in deciding whether to make a child arrangements order and, if so, in what terms;*

- *give directions to enable contested relevant factual and welfare issues to be tried as soon as possible and fairly;*

- *ensure that where domestic abuse is admitted or proven, any child arrangements order in place protects the safety and wellbeing of the child and the parent with whom the child is living, and does not expose either of them to the risk of further harm; and*

- *ensure that any interim child arrangements order (i.e. considered by the court before determination of the facts, and in the absence of admission) is only made having followed the guidance in paragraphs 25–27 below.*

  In particular, the court must be satisfied that any contact ordered with a parent who has perpetrated domestic abuse does not expose the child and/or other parent to the risk of harm and is in the best interests of the child.[88]

Notably, while factual and welfare issues are to be identified at the earliest available opportunity (which is usually the FHDRA), there is an *ongoing* duty on the court throughout the course of proceedings to consider whether domestic abuse is raised as an issue. If a party does not raise allegations until after the FHDRA, they will not necessarily be prevented from doing so further into the proceedings. A court should not simply brush these under the carpet. The court is required by PD12J to consider the nature of the allegation and its relevance, if any, to the child arrangements.

Having said that, we would urge parties alleging domestic abuse to set out their allegations as early as possible, in as much detail as possible (we have already explored the importance of doing so in the application form in the previous chapter).

Before the FHDRA

There are a number of things practitioners can do before the FHDRA to try and pre-empt issues from arising at the hearing.

The safeguarding interview

Ahead of the FHDRA, Cafcass is directed by the court to prepare a safeguarding letter. This requires them to complete short interviews with the parties (giving them the opportunity to set out their concerns); carry

---

[88] Practice Direction 12J, op. cit., at para. 5

out local authority and police checks on the family; and then set out a brief recommendation to the court on the way forward.

We are sure that views amongst lawyers will vary on the usefulness of the Cafcass safeguarding letter. The letter sets out what is largely self-reported, unverified information from both parties. In our experience, clients frequently complain about the quality of the safeguarding letter, either because they allege it misrepresents what they said during their safeguarding interview, or it does not set out their concerns as fully as they would have hoped. Increasingly, this has been because of the sheer volume of work that Cafcass receives, preventing them from being able to dedicate the appropriate time and resources to the safeguarding process.

Useful or not, PD12J makes clear that the court cannot even make a child arrangements order ('CAO') by consent or give permission for an application for a CAO to be withdrawn unless all initial safeguarding checks have been completed (except where it is satisfied that there is no risk of harm to the child and/or to the other parent in so doing).[89]

As we have mentioned earlier in this chapter, it is not at all unusual for safeguarding checks to remain outstanding at the FHDRA. Again, we suspect that this has been because of the amount of work Cafcass has to wade through. Sometimes, the Cafcass officer has been unable to contact both parents to complete their safeguarding interviews; sometimes, the order which was made on issue of the proceedings directing that they complete the safeguarding checks did not make its way to them.

There are simple, practical measures that can be taken to try and avoid miscommunication. Practitioners can contact Cafcass directly as soon as the directions on issue and allocation are received; request the details of the worker who will be completing the safeguarding checks; and send the order directly to them, highlighting the filing date for the safeguarding letter so that the worker is aware of the timescales and has plenty of notice. Practitioners should ensure that Cafcass has all the parties' contact details and times of availability to answer phone calls. If, in the days

---

[89] Practice Direction 12J, op. cit., at para. 6

leading up to the FHDRA, the client still has not had an appointment scheduled, practitioners should chase Cafcass to query when it will take place, placing pressure on them not to let the matter drift. All best efforts should be made to ensure the safeguarding interview takes place away from court, and not at court immediately prior to the FHDRA (something which happens very frequently). HHJ Dancey in *A Child (Application of PD12J)* observed that:

> "At the moment Cafcass are leaving it until the FHDRA before speaking to the parties at court. I am concerned that interviewing parents in this pressured environment rather than independently away from court risks safety issues being missed."[90]

Clients can also be encouraged to prepare for the safeguarding interview, which will be their first opportunity to engage with a professional about the issues in the case. It is not unusual for clients to become overwhelmed and flustered during the interview, failing to communicate the full extent of their experiences to the Family Court Adviser in the time available. Practitioners can encourage clients to set out a written note in advance of their interview of what they wish to tell the Family Court Adviser to ensure that nothing important is missed. It would also be sensible for clients to read the Cafcass Child Impact Assessment Framework[91] before the interview; this sets out the tools that Cafcass officers use to assess the case and the principles by which they are guided.

PD12J makes clear that if safeguarding checks are not available at the FHDRA and no other safeguarding information is available (for example, from the local authority), the court *must* adjourn the FHDRA until the checks are available.[92] If, despite all these measures to try and pre-empt issues from arising, safeguarding checks still cannot be completed ahead of the FHDRA, consideration should be given to writing to the court to invite it to vacate the hearing and re-list it if nothing can usefully be accomplished in the absence of a safeguarding letter. Privately funding parties are unlikely to want to spend their money on attending court for

---

[90] [2021] EWFC B59, at para. 139

[91] Child Impact Assessment Framework (CIAF), accessed at cafcass.gov.uk

[92] Practice Direction 12J, op. cit., at para. 12

an ineffective hearing. This may seem to be an obvious suggestion but we find that advocates are often so busy that discussions around the usefulness of any listed FHDRA may take place too late in the day. This means that any application to vacate the hearing may not reach the court for consideration in good time, and so the hearing will go ahead. As with many of the tips we set out in this book, the key is forward-planning.

The C1A Form

As we have explained in the previous chapter, the C1A supplementary form is the first opportunity either party has to shape the narrative around domestic abuse in the court proceedings. We emphasised the importance of completing it fully and in as much detail as possible. But after all that hard work, what if no one reads it?

It is not at all unusual for the C1A form to become lost in the ether prior to the FHDRA, which could potentially result in very important information being missed during Cafcass' safeguarding checks, and then falling through the gaps at the FHDRA.

Family barrister, Lucy Reed, writes on her popular *Pink Tape* blog:

> *"In the context of Practice Direction 12J and the Child Arrangements Programme, where the ethos is on early safeguarding, and on triaging cases so that they are safely conducted and so that the need for protective measures or fact finding exercises is identified early, these little forms really matter. Or they have potential to. But for some reason they are usually just ignored, especially the Respondent's C1A, which comes along later when the safeguarding train has already chugged off from the platform. That gets forgotten, like the middle sibling who nobody notices."*[93]

Safeguarding interviews completed by Cafcass are often very limited in scope and it is not unusual, as we have already noted, for clients to become overwhelmed and to fail to set out everything they would have wished to explain to the Family Court Adviser in the time available. As

---

[93] L. Reed, *'Little things sometimes matter (yes I'm a pedant)'*, Pink Tape, 27th January 2018, accessed at pinktape.co.uk

such, the C1A form – which parties will have had more time to consider and to complete carefully – can be crucial in terms of informing Cafcass' recommendations and ensuring that they are aware of the full extent of the allegations.

To avoid this being overlooked, practitioners and parties should pre-emptively send the C1A directly to the Cafcass officer ahead of the safeguarding checks being completed, and ensure that it is added to the court bundle ahead of the FHDRA.

Special measures

As practitioners, fire-fighting cases may mean that client care becomes a secondary consideration. When supporting a client who has made allegations of domestic abuse – and indeed a client facing allegations of domestic abuse – care needs to be taken to make the proceedings as predictable and transparent as possible to manage some of the stress that they will, no doubt, be suffering.

Paragraph 1.3 of Practice Direction 3AA[94], imposes a duty on the court and on *all* parties to identify at the earliest possible stage in the proceedings any party or witness who is vulnerable. Section 63 of the Domestic Abuse Act 2021 creates a presumption that where a party or witness in family proceedings is or is at risk of being a victim of domestic abuse from another party, a relative to a party or a witness in the proceedings, they are vulnerable and will need special measures (as opposed to having to justify why special measures are to be put in place).[95]

Paragraph 10 of PD12J notes that:

> *If at any stage the court is advised by any party (in the application form, or otherwise), by Cafcass or CAFCASS Cymru or otherwise that there is a need for special arrangements to protect the party or child attending any hearing, the court must ensure so far as practicable that*

---

[94] Family Procedure Rules 2010

[95] This came into force on 1st October 2021, pursuant to The Domestic Abuse Act 2021 (Commencement No. 2) Regulations 2021.

appropriate arrangements are made for the hearing (including the waiting arrangements at court prior to the hearing, and arrangements for entering and exiting the court building) and for all subsequent hearings in the case, unless it is advised and considers that these are no longer necessary. Where practicable, the court should enquire of the alleged victim of domestic abuse how best she/he wishes to participate.

This provision emphasises that there is a duty on the court – not simply on the advocate – to ensure that any required special measures are in place. This echoes the court's duty to consider making participation directions for victims of domestic abuse which is set out in r. 3A.2A[96]:

(1) Subject to paragraph (2), where it is stated that a party or witness is, or is at risk of being, a victim of domestic abuse carried out by a party, a relative of another party, or a witness in the proceedings, the court must assume that the following matters are diminished—

(a) the quality of the party's or witness's evidence;

(b) in relation to a party, their participation in the proceedings.

(2) The party or witness concerned can request that the assumption set out in paragraph (1) does not apply to them if they do not wish it to.

(3) Where the assumption set out in paragraph (1) applies, the court must consider whether it is necessary to make one or more participation directions.

The importance of the court making its own enquiries about special measures was emphasised in the decision of HHJ Ahmed in *Re A (Domestic abuse: incorrect principles applied)*.[97] That case concerned an appeal against the decision of a deputy district judge. In allowing the appeal, one of the failings identified by HHJ Ahmed was that the first-instance judge did not endeavour to make sure the mother could give her best evidence by having special measures in place. HHJ Ahmed noted that the mother cried during the litigant-in-person father's direct cross-

---

[96] Family Procedure Rules 2010

[97] [2021] EWFC B30

examination of her; there was no screen in place; there were no special measures, and there was no ground rules hearing. Although *"mother was legally represented, there was a duty on the judge to have considered whether and what special measures were necessary."*[98]

Despite what is set out in PD12J and Part 3A, practitioners will be accustomed to attending court (either virtually or in person) only to find that these measures have not been made available, or that sufficient thought has not been given to the participation of the alleged victim of domestic abuse.

Once again, the key is forward-planning and asking questions about the difficulties which could potentially arise. As a non-exhaustive list of considerations:

- Rather than just putting to the client the available options, ask the client what *they* think they would need to feel safe during the proceedings. This may involve measures that are not mentioned in the C100 or in the C1A forms, such as meeting their advocate away from court so that they do not attend the court building alone. Practitioners should think creatively around what can be done to make the client feel as comfortable as possible.

- Contact the court ahead of the hearing to check that any requested special measures such as screens or separate waiting rooms have been put in place.

- Check that the court has booked an interpreter, if one has been requested.

- Consider the possible issues that could arise in Covid-19 times. Many courts do not allow parties to enter the court building more than fifteen or thirty minutes prior to the court hearing. This raises the risk of the parties coming into contact whilst waiting in the queue outside. One suggestion would be to contact the court

---

[98] ibid., at para. 25

- ahead of time to request that the client be permitted to enter the building earlier than the local court protocol allows.

- If the hearing is taking place remotely, how can special measures be facilitated? If the client is dialling in by telephone, is their number confidential when it appears on the screen? Can the court facilitate 'virtual screens' whereby the client can be seen by the judge but not the other party? Some of these issues could be dealt with by joining the hearing link earlier than the listed hearing time and raising these queries with the court clerk.

- If the client is attending remotely via video link, does their video background have any identifying details that might give away a confidential location? Do they know how to blur their background on the relevant platform? Would it be safer for them to attend from their solicitor's offices or from their counsel's chambers?

- Some courts are in the habit of sending hearing links just moments before the listed hearing. Try and obtain a hearing link several working days before the hearing to ensure adequate time is available for the client to test the link, or at least establish the window of time during which the link will be sent to avoid unnecessary anxiety on the client's part.

- If the client struggles with technology, should arrangements be made for them to attend from their solicitor's offices or from their counsel's chambers?

The Family Justice Council has prepared extremely helpful guidance on special measures in remote and hybrid hearings[99], with a comprehensive checklist of considerations for proceedings in which domestic abuse is an issue. Practitioners should take clients through this and work out a clear plan of action for the FHDRA and for subsequent hearings.

---

[99] Family Justice Council, *'Safety from Domestic Abuse and Special Measures in Remote and Hybrid Hearings'*, November 2020, accessed at judiciary.uk

During the FHDRA

Interim contact

The issue which, in our experience, most frequently arises at the FHDRA is interim contact. Very often, one parent has stopped or severely limited contact with the other parent. The other parent hopes that contact can be progressed at the first hearing. Very often, that parent is disappointed.

Interim child arrangements prior to determination of allegations of domestic abuse are governed by paragraphs 25 to 27 of PD12J.

> 25. *Where the court gives directions for a fact-finding hearing, or where disputed allegations of domestic abuse are otherwise undetermined, the court should not make an interim child arrangements order unless it is satisfied that it is in the interests of the child to do so and that the order would not expose the child or the other parent to an unmanageable risk of harm (bearing in mind the impact which domestic abuse against a parent can have on the emotional well-being of the child, the safety of the other parent and the need to protect against domestic abuse including controlling or coercive behaviour).*
>
> 26. *In deciding any interim child arrangements question the court should–*
>
>   a) *take into account the matters set out in section 1(3) of the Children Act 1989 or section 1(4) of the Adoption and Children Act 2002 ('the welfare check-list'), as appropriate; and*
>
>   b) *give particular consideration to the likely effect on the child, and on the care given to the child by the parent who has made the allegation of domestic abuse, of any contact and any risk of harm, whether physical, emotional or psychological, which the child and that parent is likely to suffer as a consequence of making or declining to make an order.*

27. *Where the court is considering whether to make an order for interim contact, it should in addition consider –*

   a) *the arrangements required to ensure, as far as possible, that any risk of harm to the child and the parent who is at any time caring for the child is minimised and that the safety of the child and the parties is secured; and in particular:*

      i. *whether the contact should be supervised or supported, and if so, where and by whom; and*

      ii. *the availability of appropriate facilities for that purpose;*

   b) *if direct contact is not appropriate, whether it is in the best interests of the child to make an order for indirect contact; and*

   c) *whether contact will be beneficial for the child.*

Paragraph 25 makes clear that where a fact-finding hearing is on the horizon or where there are allegations of domestic abuse which are yet to be settled, there is a *presumption* that the court should not make an interim child arrangements order *unless* it is satisfied that it is in the interests of the child to do so and that the order would not expose the child or the other parent to an unmanageable risk of harm.

Paragraph 26 requires the court to consider the welfare checklist at s1(3) of the *Children Act 1989* when determining interim child arrangements, as well as the likely effect on the child and on the care given to them by the parent who has alleged the domestic abuse, of any contact. The welfare checklist includes factors such as any harm which the child has suffered or is at risk of suffering; and how capable each of the parents are of meeting the child's needs. It is difficult to see how the court would be able to assess these matters prior to a fact-finding hearing and prior to there being fuller risk assessment. This often leaves the court in the position of being unable to make interim orders for direct contact until it determines where the truth lies.

Decisions at an interim stage are necessarily based on incomplete information. A helpful illustrative case of the difficulties posed in respect of interim child arrangements is the recent case of *A Child (Application of PD12J)*[100]. This concerned an appeal against the interim decision of a district judge directing that the mother in that case return with the children from the North of England (where the mother was living with the children in a refuge) to Dorset, where there would be an interim shared care arrangement with the father. If the mother failed to return, the judge directed that there would be a transfer of residence from the mother to the father.

In that case, the mother made very serious allegations against the father, including that he was controlling and coercive, and that he had been sexually abusive, laying on top of her and holding her down while having sex so she could not breathe. The mother also alleged – and the father admitted – that he had lied to the mother about being HIV+, and she had not learned about this until 7 years into the marriage and after the birth of all three children.

In considering the appeal, HHJ Dancey noted that the "*acutely difficult question*" posed by the appeal "*is the balance to be struck by the court between (a) the potential harm identified by PD12J of making orders that may place children at risk of the consequences of domestic abuse and (b) the emotional harm and potential relationship damage that may be caused by unilateral removal a considerable distance away from the family home and cessation of contact.*"[101]

HHJ Dancey suggested during submissions that:

> "*the framework of analysis posted by Jackson LJ (in the different context of care proceedings) in* Re F (A Child) (Placement Order: Proportionality) [2018] EWCA Civ 2761 *might be a useful way of addressing the balancing exercise, adapted to the needs of any given case:*
>
> a) *What is the type of harm that might arise (for present purposes, putting the mother's case at its highest)?*

---

[100] op. cit.

[101] ibid., at para. 120

> b) *What is the likelihood of it arising?*
>
> c) *What would be the consequences in terms of severity of harm if it happened?*
>
> d) *Can the risks of harm happening be reduced or mitigated so that they are manageable (including in this case by the making of protective measures)?*
>
> e) *What does a comparative evaluation of the advantages and disadvantages of each option (here, return or not, contact or not) say about the best interests of the children, having regard also to the need to protect a parent vulnerable to abuse?*
>
> f) *Is the outcome proposed proportionate?"*[102]

HHJ Dancey also noted that while the mother's case should be taken at its highest, that "*does not mean… the court is bound to accept everything that is said without any sort of critical analysis.*"[103] He observes:

> "*The court is entitled (indeed I would suggest required) at an interim stage to consider the circumstances around the allegations including:*
>
> a) *the seriousness of the allegations and the harm that might result;*
>
> b) *whether there is already evidence from other sources which supports or undermines the allegations;*
>
> c) *the consistency or otherwise of the allegations (making allowance for the fact that it is in the nature of domestic abuse that accounts are often given piecemeal and incrementally, especially in relation to allegations of sexual abuse which may be delayed because of embarrassment, shame or simply thinking 'I won't be believed');*

---

[102] ibid., at para. 122

[103] ibid., at para. 123

d) possible motivations for making allegations;

e) how the children are presenting and what they are saying."[104]

In that case, HHJ Dancey allowed the appeal and set aside the order, concluding that:

> *"While allowing for the fact that the district judge's judgment was extempore and that perfection is not expected, it does seem to me that in respect of the following his approach was wrong:*
>
> *a) while he was entitled to take a critical or even sceptical approach to the allegations of domestic abuse, it was not open to the district judge effectively to dismiss them summarily or set them entirely to one side for the purpose of making interim orders;*
>
> *b) as a result the district judge did not engage with PD12J until very much as an after thought once he had determined the interim orders he would make;*
>
> *c) the district judge dismissed the question of risk without sufficient analysis or information, particularly on the more subtle question of coercive or controlling behaviour and the potential emotional and psychological impact;*
>
> *d) the district judge gave insufficient weight to the Cafcass recommendations, based on limited information though they were, and failed to explain why he was departing from them in such a wholescale way;*
>
> *e) while addressing the welfare checklist in relation to the question of removal, the district judge did not apply it holistically in relation to the question of return to the father, or spending time with him."*[105]

---

[104] ibid., at para. 124

[105] ibid., at para. 130

The practical reality is that the parent seeking contact may find themselves in the unsatisfactory position of being unable to progress meaningful contact until after the fact-finding hearing is completed, a section 7 report has been completed and we are at a DRA. The balance of power at the beginning of proceedings usually tips in favour of the parent advancing the allegations and resisting contact, even though those allegations have not yet been determined. Even if everything runs smoothly, it can take many, many months to get to a DRA. This means that the parent facing the allegations could potentially have to wait a very long time before the court would even *consider* direct contact progressing. In our experience, it is not unusual for clients to set out a detailed list of the contact arrangements they hope to achieve, expecting that the court will simply direct these at the FHDRA. Advocates acting for the party facing the allegations must ensure that they manage their client's expectations ahead of the FHDRA.

The court will usually be guided by the recommendations in the Cafcass safeguarding letter – albeit this is usually based on partial, self-reported information – which will provide a helpful starting point when having pre-hearing discussions with the client about what might happen at the FHDRA. If Cafcass has identified serious risks that are to be assessed which are relevant to child arrangements, they may take the conservative position of saying that they cannot support any direct contact until the relevant facts have been determined. Although Cafcass's recommendations are simply recommendations, it would be a bold tribunal indeed who would direct contact against professional advice, unless there have been serious flaws in Cafcass's risk screening process during the safeguarding process which render their recommendations questionable.

Clients have to be prepared for the worst-case scenario: if the other party does not agree to direct contact progressing until the court has determined the relevant facts and assessed risk, and Cafcass takes the same view, this may mean that contact cannot move forward until after a fact-finding hearing (and that is predicated on the assumption that adverse findings are not made at that hearing). If this looks to be the trajectory of the case, advocates should focus on identifying alternative means of contact to which the court would be more amenable, such as the sharing of pictures and regular updates about the children, or indirect contact by way of gifts, cards and letters.

Finally, as we have noted above, many FHDRAs are currently being listed before legal advisers sitting alone, who 'triage' matters at the first hearing, freeing up valuable sitting time for lay justices. This means that at many FHDRAs, the legal adviser can only endorse an agreed order and cannot determine matters such as interim contact. It is imperative that this is explained to clients ahead of the FHDRA, particularly if they are seeking interim contact, so that they are not shocked and disappointed when this becomes clear to them in the hearing itself.

In such circumstances, advocates may wish to consider inviting the court to list an interim contested contact hearing before lay justices so that the client does not have to wait until the fact-finding hearing or the DRA before contact arrangements can be revisited. However, given the delays in court listing, it may be many months before such a hearing can be accommodated in any event. We would also reiterate what has already been said above about the court being guided by professional advice. Thought would need to be given to prospects of success at any contested interim hearing; the court will still be without the benefit of a fact-finding judgment or a professional risk assessment. Is it likely that they will depart from the recommendations of Cafcass and direct contact above and beyond what Cafcass considers to be safe at this stage? If the client is privately funding, are they willing to lose money over an additional hearing that may be unsuccessful? If the client is proposing that evidence be heard at such a hearing, are they aware of the risk of adverse findings being made against them at this early stage?

It is clear that practitioners will need to have uncomfortable conversations with clients about the limits to what can be achieved within a system beset by chronic delays.

The need for a fact-finding hearing

Paragraphs 16 to 17 of PD12J deal with the need for a fact-finding hearing. For ease, they are set out here:

16. The court should determine as soon as possible whether it is necessary to conduct a fact-finding hearing in relation to any disputed allegation of domestic abuse –

a) in order to provide a factual basis for any welfare report or for assessment of the factors set out in paragraphs 36 and 37 below;

b) in order to provide a basis for an accurate assessment of risk;

c) before it can consider any final welfare-based order(s) in relation to child arrangements; or

d) before it considers the need for a domestic abuse-related Activity (such as a Domestic Violence Perpetrator Programme (DVPP)).

17. In determining whether it is necessary to conduct a fact-finding hearing, the court should consider –

a) the views of the parties and of Cafcass or CAFCASS Cymru;

b) whether there are admissions by a party which provide a sufficient factual basis on which to proceed;

c) if a party is in receipt of legal aid, whether the evidence required to be provided to obtain legal aid provides a sufficient factual basis on which to proceed;

d) whether there is other evidence available to the court that provides a sufficient factual basis on which to proceed;

e) whether the factors set out in paragraphs 36 and 37 below can be determined without a fact-finding hearing;

f) the nature of the evidence required to resolve disputed allegations;

g) whether the nature and extent of the allegations, if proved, would be relevant to the issue before the court; and

h) *whether a separate fact-finding hearing would be necessary and proportionate in all the circumstances of the case.*

Notably, paragraphs 16 and 17 refer to whether it is "necessary" to conduct a fact-finding hearing, which is a higher test than whether it is simply "desirable" to conduct a fact-finding hearing.

The Court of Appeal in *Re H-N & ors* devoted much of the judgment to exploring the need for and the scope of any fact-finding hearing. The Court noted the need for "*procedural proportionality at all times, both before and during any fact-finding process*"[106]. The Court also referred to the President's Guidance, '*The Road Ahead*'[107]:

> "*If the Family Court is to have any chance of delivering on the needs of children or adults who need protection from abuse, or of their families for a timely determination of applications, there will need to be <u>a very radical reduction in the amount of time</u> that the court affords to each hearing. Parties appearing before the court should expect the issues to be limited only to those which it is <u>necessary</u> to determine to dispose of the case, and for oral evidence or oral submissions to be cut down only to that which it is necessary for the court to hear.*"

The Court went on to offer the following guidance[108]:

> "*i. The first stage is to consider the nature of the allegations and the extent to which it is likely to be relevant in deciding whether to make a child arrangements order and if so in what terms (PD12J.5).*
>
> *ii. In deciding whether to have a finding of fact hearing the court should have in mind its purpose (PD12J.16) which is, in broad terms, to provide a basis of assessment of risk and therefore the impact of the alleged abuse on the child or children.*
>
> *iii. Careful consideration must be given to PD12J.17 as to whether it is 'necessary' to have a finding of fact hearing, including whether there*

---

[106] *Re H-N & ors*, op. cit., at para. 36

[107] A. McFarlane, '*The Road Ahead*', June 2020, accessed at: judiciary.uk

[108] *Re H-N & ors*, op. cit., at para. 37

> is other evidence which provides a sufficient factual basis to proceed and importantly, the relevance to the issue before the court if the allegations are proved.
>
> iv. Under PD12J.17 (h) the court has to consider whether a separate fact-finding hearing is 'necessary and proportionate'. The court and the parties should have in mind as part of its analysis both the overriding objective and the President's Guidance as set out in 'The Road Ahead'."

The guidance above is not new and should not be surprising. These are things that the Family Court should already be doing. Are the allegations relevant to the child's welfare or are they simply attempts by the parties to "mud-sling"? Does the party facing the allegations admit, even in a limited way, to any of the alleged behaviours? If the allegations are proved, where does this take us? If proved, do the allegations establish that the perpetrator is a risk of harm to the child or to the other parent? Is there other evidence available which could circumvent the need for a fact-finding hearing, for example criminal convictions?

However, there is a clear tension at the heart of *Re H-N & ors* between managing cases expeditiously and in line with the overriding objective, and allowing parties to raise the allegations which they believe will give the court a full and nuanced picture of the abuse being alleged. We suspect that we are likely to see matters listed for longer fact-finding hearings as judges take a more cautious approach to limiting the allegations which can be raised by the parties. This will have a knock-on effect on the court system itself, as courts that are already overstretched struggle to accommodate lengthier fact-finding hearings.

Post-*Re H-N & ors*, we have already seen some judges being criticised from limiting the number of allegations placed before the court:

- In *Re A (Domestic abuse: incorrect principles applied)*[109], one of the criticisms levelled at the judgment under appeal was that the mother was restricted by lay justices initially to just raising one allegation (an allegation of physical violence). Following a

---

[109] *Re A (Domestic abuse: incorrect principles applied)*, op. cit., at para. 26

successful appeal to a circuit judge, this was increased to four allegations, which was still considered by HHJ Ahmed to be too restrictive. HHJ Ahmed noted:

> "It was common for judges to impose such limitations on the number of allegations. However, the restriction made it difficult for the mother to present a case properly on the basis of a pattern of behaviour over a period of time. Nuanced appreciation of the mother's allegations was lost."

- In *AA v BB*[110], Judd J allowed an appeal after the first-instance recorder considered large chunks of the mother's evidence to be irrelevant or inadmissible and prevented her from relying on them. Part of his decision-making had been driven by a concern that the fact-finding hearing not become too lengthy. Judd J disagreed and considered that the allegations *were* relevant, for example, allegations that the father had hit one of the children several times and forced mother to have sex on several occasions. She set aside the decision and directed that mother file a statement setting out her allegations and father file a response.

The key tension in *Re H-N & ors* is perhaps best illustrated by the following observation of the Court of Appeal:

> "It is the responsibility of the individual judge or bench of magistrates in each case to set a proportionate timetable and to maintain control of the court process where it has been determined that a fact-finding hearing is necessary. It is, however, our expectation that, in cases where an alleged pattern of coercive and/or controlling behaviour falls for determination, and the court has made that issue its primary focus, the need to determine a range of subsidiary date-specific factual allegations will cease to be 'necessary' (unless any particular factual allegation is so

---

[110] [2021] EWHC 1822. See also: M. Jaganmohan, 'What does AA v BB tell us about the treatment of domestic abuse since Re H-N?', The Transparency Project Blog, 10th August 2021, accessed at transparencyproject.org.uk

serious that it justifies determination irrespective of any alleged pattern of coercive and/or controlling behaviour). "[111]

Judges find themselves in a difficult position: they need to case manage robustly so that matters are not unnecessarily prolonged and so that any fact-finding hearing is proportionate to the issues in dispute. However, if they case manage *too* robustly, they risk opening themselves up to appeal by restricting alleged victims of abuse from being able to paint an accurate picture to the court of what they have experienced.

A note of caution

Since the onset of the Covid-19 pandemic, some courts are not listing FHDRAs at all. Instead, directions are being dealt with on paper, and section 7 reports and DRAs being timetabled without any explicit consideration of the allegations of domestic abuse and how the court should deal with them. This could lead to the unfortunate position where, at the DRA several months into proceedings, a section 7 report has been completed which makes certain recommendations, but one or both of the parties raise concerns that there are undetermined allegations of domestic abuse which have not been factored into the risk analysis. In the worst-case scenario, the court may decide at that late stage that, in fact, a fact-finding hearing is needed. This could lead to many more months of delay that could have been avoided had there been an opportunity to raise this at a FHDRA.

Practitioners acting for clients who are making allegations of domestic abuse that are likely to be relevant to child arrangements and are likely to require a fact-finding hearing should act swiftly. They must seek to return the matter to court for directions at the earliest opportunity so that the issue of domestic abuse can be explicitly considered and directions made accordingly. If they do not, there is a risk that the issue of domestic abuse is brushed over entirely. If, at a later stage, the client then wishes to invite the court to determine the allegations by way of a fact-finding hearing,

---

[111] *Re H-N & ors*, op. cit., at para. 56

the court may take the view that this issue should have been raised much earlier and any further delay would not be in the interests of the child.

It is good practice to recite on the face of the order at the first hearing that domestic abuse has been raised as an issue which is/is not likely to be relevant to any decision of the court relating to the child; and what the court has decided to do in order to deal with these allegations. There is a helpful form of wording in the President's Compendium of Standard Family Orders (*Order 7.4: Private Law Directions at FHDRA (allegations of domestic abuse)*), which appears to have been drafted with paragraph 14 of PD12J in mind. This allows any future judge or panel of justices to check that domestic abuse has been considered.

Checklist for the FHDRA

If issues of domestic abuse have been raised, have you considered the following?

- ☐ Has Cafcass received the order directing that safeguarding checks be completed? Are they aware of the filing date by which the safeguarding checks are to be completed?

- ☐ Does Cafcass have the parties' contact details and times of availability for a telephone interview. If a party requires an interpreter, have arrangements been made for an interpreter to be present at the telephone interview?

- ☐ Does Cafcass have the C1A form/s?

- ☐ What does the safeguarding letter recommend? If the client is seeking contact and facing allegations of abuse, manage the client's expectations about what can realistically be accomplished at the FHDRA. Explore the interim arrangements that will be placed before the court, including any proposals for indirect contact.

- ☐ If the safeguarding checks are outstanding, should an application be made to adjourn the FHDRA until they are completed? Can anything be accomplished at the FHDRA in the absence of the safeguarding checks?

☐ Is the FHDRA before a legal adviser sitting alone? Explain to the client the implications of this.

☐ If the FHDRA is listed before a legal adviser sitting alone, should the court be invited to list the matter before lay justices if it is likely that there will be disputed issues which need determining?

☐ If the FHDRA is before a legal adviser sitting alone, does the client invite the court to list the matter for a contested interim contact hearing? What are the client's prospects of success at this hearing? Have they been appraised of the pros and cons of inviting the court to list a contested interim contact hearing?

☐ Has the court dispensed with the need for a FHDRA and timetabled straight through to a DRA? Does the matter need to be returned to court urgently so that consideration can be given to how any allegations of domestic abuse are to be investigated?

☐ Is a fact-finding hearing needed? Are the allegations relevant to the child's welfare? If proved, would they establish that the perpetrator is a risk of harm to the child or the other parent?

☐ Is there other evidence which would deal with the allegations without the need for a fact-finding hearing?

☐ If there is an ongoing criminal investigation or criminal proceedings, when will the outcome of these be known? Would the outcome obviate the need for a fact-finding hearing?

☐ Does the person facing the allegations make any admissions to the allegations?

☐ Is it clear on the face of the order made at the FHDRA that domestic abuse has been raised as an issue? Is it clear on the face of the order how the court has decided to approach these allegations of domestic abuse?

CHAPTER FIVE

THE FACT-FINDING HEARING

The fact-finding hearing is arguably the most stressful hearing of the court proceedings. The party alleging abuse is forced to re-hash the allegations in forensic detail in the court arena. The allegations may be extremely sensitive and extremely painful, and the cross-examining advocate is duty-bound to put their client's case robustly. This may involve putting to the alleged victim that they are lying, acting maliciously, struggling with their mental health, or whatever the advocate's instructions might be.

Campaigners have criticised advocates for perpetuating myths about domestic abuse by posing certain questions to the alleged victim in cross-examination, for example: why did you not report the abuse earlier? Why did you stay in the relationship if you were being abused?

Whilst these questions seem distasteful given what we know about domestic abuse more broadly and the many reasons why victims may remain silent and may remain in an abusive relationship, nonetheless they are likely to be questions that need to be put by the cross-examining advocate. No matter how uncomfortable the advocate may find these lines of enquiry to be, they must act fearlessly in their client's interests. It is then a matter for the opposing advocate to challenge those arguments, and for the court to place appropriate weight on those submissions. This is why domestic abuse training for judges and for advocates is imperative so that they can recognise and interrogate myths and assumptions being advanced in court, rather than expecting them not to be advanced in the first place.

Having said that, the cross-examining advocate can put their client's case fully and clearly without being unintentionally abusive and without contributing to the alleged victim becoming re-traumatised. There is a difference between robust advocacy and the perpetuation of abuse.

Should you be conducting the fact-finding hearing?

As a preliminary consideration, this is the first question that we would want advocates to ask themselves. Fact-finding hearings can involve some of the most serious, some of the most troubling allegations imaginable; many fact-finding hearings are not for the faint of heart. For barristers, Core Duty 7 of their Code of Conduct requires barristers to provide a competent standard of work and service to the client, and rC21.8 states that barristers must not accept instructions to act in a particular matter if they are not competent to handle the particular matter or otherwise do not have enough experience to handle the matter. Similarly, for solicitors, paras. 3.2 and 3.3 of the SRA's Code of Conduct for Solicitors, RELs and RFLs, sets out that service to clients must be competent and that solicitors must maintain their competence to carry out their role and keep their professional knowledge and skills up to date.

Competency is ultimately a matter for the individual lawyer's judgment. We would suggest that junior practitioners speak to someone more senior in their firm or chambers about whether or not a case is a suitable one for them to take on before accepting the instructions. Some of the sorts of allegations which might give practitioners pause for thought might include rape, attempted strangulation or attempted suffocation. Do you have the skills and the experience to cross-examine where there are disputed allegations of this sort? These allegations are routinely heard by deputy district judges and district judges, but that does not make them any less serious. The findings made in the Family Court may have a bearing on any criminal prosecution and so it is imperative that the allegations are managed appropriately in the family jurisdiction.

We also have some suggestions for family lawyers when considering how they can build their competence. The Family Law Bar Association and the Inns of Court College of Advocacy have recently started to roll out their 'Advocacy and the Vulnerable' training programme, modelled upon a similar programme used to train the Criminal Bar. We would urge members of the Family Bar to make use of this training to improve consistency of practice across the board. We would also urge practitioners to familiarise themselves with the Advocate's Gateway's Toolkit 12: 'Vulnerable Witnesses in the Family Courts'.[112]

Directions for a fact-finding hearing

When thinking about the fact-finding hearing, we first need to consider what evidence is needed and what directions should be considered before we get to the fact-finding hearing. Paragraph 19 of PD12J sets out a helpful list of considerations for the court:

> *Where the court considers that a fact-finding hearing is necessary, it must give directions as to how the proceedings are to be conducted to ensure that the matters in issue are determined as soon as possible, fairly and proportionately, and within the capabilities of the parties. In particular it should consider –*
>
> *a) what are the key facts in dispute;*
>
> *b) whether it is necessary for the fact-finding to take place at a separate (and earlier) hearing than the welfare hearing;*
>
> *c) whether the key facts in dispute can be contained in a schedule or a table (known as a Scott Schedule) which sets out what the applicant complains of or alleges, what the respondent says in relation to each individual allegation or complaint; the allegations in the schedule should be focused on the factual issues to be tried; and if so, whether it is practicable for this schedule to be completed at the first hearing, with the assistance of the judge;*
>
> *d) what evidence is required in order to determine the existence of coercive, controlling or threatening behaviour, or of any other form of domestic abuse;*

---

[112] The Advocates Gateway, '*Vulnerable witnesses and parties in the family courts: Toolkit 13*', 2nd September 2019, accessed at theadvocatesgateway.org

e) *directing the parties to file written statements giving details of such behaviour and of any response;*

f) *whether documents are required from third parties such as the police, health services or domestic abuse support services and giving directions for those documents to be obtained;*

g) *whether oral evidence may be required from third parties and if so, giving directions for the filing of written statements from such third parties;*

h) *where (for example in cases of abandonment) third parties from whom documents are to be obtained are abroad, how to obtain those documents in good time for the hearing, and who should be responsible for the costs of obtaining those documents;*

i) *whether any other evidence is required to enable the court to decide the key issues and giving directions for that evidence to be provided;*

j) *what evidence the alleged victim of domestic abuse is able to give and what support the alleged victim may require at the fact-finding hearing in order to give that evidence;*

k) *in cases where the alleged victim of domestic abuse is unable for reasons beyond their control to be present at the hearing (for example, abandonment cases where the abandoned spouse remains abroad), what measures should be taken to ensure that that person's best evidence can be put before the court. Where video-link is not available, the court should consider alternative technological or other methods which may be utilised to allow that person to participate in the proceedings;*

l) *what support the alleged perpetrator may need in order to have a reasonable opportunity to challenge the evidence; and*

m) *whether a pre-hearing review would be useful prior to the fact-finding hearing to ensure directions have been complied with and all the required evidence is available.*

Scott Schedules

If the parties are agreed and/or the court directs that a fact-finding hearing is needed, or that further information is required before a determination can be made about the need for a fact-finding hearing, the advocates should turn their minds to how best this information can be presented. In light of the observations in both *Re H-N & ors* and *F v M*, there has been a cultural shift away from the use of Scott Schedules. As we have already discussed earlier in this book, those judgments cast doubt on the ongoing usefulness of Scott Schedules, and indeed raised the concern that Scott Schedules could be an active hindrance to fairness and due process. Despite this, Scott Schedules are likely not to disappear altogether, particularly in cases where a pattern of behaviour is not alleged and there are isolated incidents which require determination. However, if Scott Schedules are to be used, great care needs to be taken to avoid "*slavish adherence to Schedules*".[113]

We are likely to see courts and advocates experimenting with different ways of presenting allegations which allow the court to appreciate their nuances. Various options were floated in submissions made before the Court of Appeal in *Re H-N & ors*, including: a 'threshold' type document, similar to what is used in care proceedings; formal pleadings by way of particulars of claim; and a narrative statement in prescribed form.[114]

One possible way forward is that suggested by Poole J in *Re JK (A Child) (Domestic Abuse; Finding of Fact Hearing)*[115], namely that in addition to witness evidence, it would be helpful to have concise statements on behalf of each party including:

- A summary of the nature of the relationship;

---

[113] *Re JK (A Child) (Domestic Abuse: Finding of Fact Hearing)* [2021] EWHC 1367, at para. 28

[114] *Re HN & ors*, op. cit., at para. 48

[115] *Re JK (A Child) (Domestic Abuse: Finding of Fact Hearing)*, op. cit., at para. 28

- A list of the forms of domestic abuse that the evidence is said to establish;

- A list of key specific incidents said to be probative of a pattern of coercion and/or control;

- A list of any other specific incidents so serious that they justify determination irrespective of any alleged pattern of coercive and/or controlling behaviour.

Whatever the mechanism used by the parties to frame the allegations, the emphasis needs to be on setting out the full canvas of evidence so that the court can get an accurate picture of the dynamics in the parties' relationship.

Supporting witness statements and third-party evidence

The following non-exhaustive list sets out the types of third-party evidence which may assist the court in determining the disputed allegations at a fact-finding hearing:

- Supporting witness evidence from individuals who have observed specific incidents or abusive behaviours, or who have witnessed the impact of the alleged abuse on the alleged victim. Statements from individuals who are not family and friends are likely to be considered more compelling, but that should not discourage clients from seeking to rely on the evidence of family and friends, if that evidence is relevant;

- Screenshots of texts, call logs, Whatsapp messages or other social media communications, particularly if sent contemporaneously;

- Local authority assessments, such as s47 enquiries or Child and Family Assessments;

- Bank statements or other financial information;

- Information from the local authority Housing team, for instance if there have been reports or complaints by concerned neighbours;

- Police disclosure, if there have been police call-outs or reports to the police of the alleged abusive behaviours;

- Records of hospital admissions or GP appointments (for example, if the party alleging abuse has sustained injuries and sought treatment);

- Letters from domestic abuse support services in respect of their involvement with the alleged victim; any allegations shared with them; and any support offered. While such documents may simply set out the self-reported allegations of the parties, they will be relevant to the parties' credibility and consistency in that the allegations have been repeated to multiple individuals or agencies.

It is imperative that the proceedings are carefully managed because hearing from additional witnesses or requesting documents from third-party agencies will inevitably prolong the proceedings. As advocates, we must advise clients firmly about what added value their supporting evidence has and whether any associated delay caused by obtaining that evidence is worth it. We must also be prepared to resist applications to rely on evidence which we suspect will not assist the court and will simply add to the 'white noise' around the proceedings.

Special measures and cross-examination

Practice Direction 12J goes on to set out the following in respect of fact-finding hearings:

> 28. *While ensuring that the allegations are properly put and responded to, the fact-finding hearing or other hearing can be an inquisitorial (or investigative) process, which at all times must protect the interests of all involved. At the fact-finding hearing or other hearing –*
>
> - *each party can be asked to identify what questions they wish to ask of the other party, and to set out or confirm in sworn evidence their version of the disputed key facts; and*
>
> - *the judge should be prepared where necessary and appropriate to conduct the questioning of the witnesses on behalf of the parties, focusing on the key issues in the case.*
>
> 29. *The court should, wherever practicable, make findings of fact as to the nature and degree of any domestic abuse which is established and its effect on the child, the child's parents and any other relevant person. The court must record its findings in writing in a Schedule to the relevant order, and the court office must serve a copy of this order on the parties. A copy of any record of findings of fact or of admissions must be sent by the court office to any officer preparing a report under Section 7 of the 1989 Act.*

Paragraph 28 emphasises that the fact-finding process "*at all times must protect the interests of all involved*" [emphasis added]. This makes clear that the priority is not simply protecting the interests of the party who is alleging abuse. The implications for the party facing the allegations of abuse are also huge. The court cannot just take at face-value what is said by the alleged victim; it must look closely at the allegations, at the available evidence, and assess the parties' credibility before taking a view. Again, it may seem distasteful not to take an alleged victim of abuse at their word, but the family justice system must operate on evidence rather than on untested allegations.

However, how can we test those allegations whilst keeping the alleged victim safe from re-traumatisation?

We have already discussed special measures in this book in the chapter on FHDRAs. Much of that will apply here as well. It goes without saying that very careful thought needs to be given to the participation of the alleged victim in the fact-finding hearing. The advocates and the court need to appreciate that sometimes the worst evidence can come from the alleged victim themselves. It is now well-understood that the process of giving evidence can be extremely traumatising for an alleged victim of abuse. *Giving* evidence could result in them re-living the abuse, affecting the quality of the evidence that they give, while *listening* to the evidence of the alleged abuser could result in them questioning their own narrative.

All best endeavours need to be made to understand and to mitigate the impact of trauma on the quality of the alleged victim's evidence and on their ability to process the abuse. The court needs to appreciate that matters such as witness demeanour and body language – factors which are routinely taken into account when assessing the parties' credibility – require a far more nuanced approach in cases of domestic abuse where trauma will undoubtedly impact upon the alleged victim's presentation.

The Family Justice Council's guidance on special measures in remote and hybrid hearings to which we have already referred notes that fully remote hearings may not be suitable for a fact-finding, and a hybrid or fully attended hearing should be considered.[116] There are obvious reasons for this, for example: the quality of the parties' evidence may be diminished over a video link, or the parties (particularly the party alleging abuse) may benefit from the moral support of having their legal representative by their side at court.

We would urge extreme caution if there is any suggestion that the alleged abuser cross-examine the alleged victim directly if they are not legally represented, unless the alleged victim has made very clear that they have no difficulty with being cross-examined directly (and this should be recorded on the face of the order for the avoidance of all doubt). We have already discussed in the previous chapter the appeal in *Re A (Domestic abuse: incorrect principles applied),* in which HHJ Ahmed was critical of the first-instance judge for his failure to put special measures in place to

---

[116] '*Safety from Domestic Abuse and Special Measures in Remote and Hybrid Hearings*', op. cit.

ensure that the mother gave her best evidence.[117] In that case, the mother had been directly cross-examined by the litigant-in-person father and was crying during her evidence.

The Practice Direction notes that it is entirely appropriate to request that a party prepare questions in advance (which can then be provided to the judge to consider whether they are relevant and to then put them to the witness) in lieu of cross-examining the witness directly. It is also appropriate for the judge to cross-examine on behalf of any unrepresented party, albeit this is far from an ideal solution. It would be prudent to explain to the client in advance that the judge may assist litigants-in-person in this way so that the client does not think the judge is biased or on the other party's 'side'.

We would also note that s65 of the Domestic Abuse Act 2021 will be introducing new prohibitions on alleged victims of domestic abuse and alleged perpetrators of domestic abuse being able to cross-examine one another. We will not go into these provisions in any great detail given that, at the time of writing, they are yet to come into force. Broadly speaking:

- If one of the parties has been convicted of, cautioned for, or charged with a "specified offence", they cannot directly cross-examine in person a witness who is the victim or alleged victim of that offence (and vice versa). A specified offence is an offence which is specified in, or of a description specified, in regulations made by the Lord Chancellor.

- If one of the parties is subject to an on-notice protective injunction, they cannot directly cross-examine in person a witness who is protected by that injunction (and vice versa).

- Where "specified evidence" is adduced that a witness has been the victim of domestic abuse carried out by a party to the proceedings, that party cannot directly cross-examine the witness in person. Similarly, if "specified evidence" is adduced that a

---

[117] *Re A (Domestic abuse: incorrect principles applied)*, op. cit., at para. 25.

person who is a party to the proceedings has been the victim of domestic abuse carried out by a witness, they cannot directly cross-examine in person the witness. "Specified evidence" means evidence specified, or of a description specified, in regulations made by the Lord chancellor.

- If none of the above sections operate to prevent a party from cross-examining a witness in person, the court may direct that the party be prohibited from cross-examining the witness in person if:

    i. The quality of the evidence given by the witness is likely to be diminished by cross-examination conducted by the party in person, and would be likely to be improved if there was a prohibition on that cross-examination, **or**

    ii. The cross-examination of the witness by the party in person would cause significant distress to the witness or the party, and that distress is likely to be more significant than would be the case if the witness were cross-examined other than by that party in person.

    In addition to at least one of the above conditions being met, it should not be contrary to the interests of justice to direct that a party be prohibited from cross-examining the witness in person.

    Section 65 sets out the matters to which the court must have regard when determining whether the 'quality condition' or 'significant distress condition' is met.

Section 65 also sets out alternatives to cross-examination in person:

- If the court cannot find satisfactory alternative means for the witness to be cross-examined or of obtaining evidence that the witness might have given under cross-examination, the court must invite the party to arrange for a qualified legal representative to act for them for the purpose of cross-examining the witness and give them a deadline by which they must do this.

- If, by that date, the party notifies the court that no qualified legal representative is to act for them for the purpose of cross-examining the witness or no notification has been received by the court and it appears to the court that no qualified legal representative is to act for the party for the purpose of cross-examining the witness, the court must consider whether it is necessary in the interests of justice for the witness to be cross-examined by a qualified legal representative appointed by the court to represent the interests of the party.

- If the court decides it is, the court must appoint a qualified legal representative to cross-examine the witness in the interests of the party.

We do not yet have a date for when this section will come into force, albeit the commencement schedule says it will be in Spring 2022.

Ground rules hearings

Thought should be given to whether a separate ground rules hearing is needed before the fact-finding hearing, or whether ground rules could be dealt with as a discrete 'housekeeping' matter at the beginning of the fact-finding hearing.

Paragraph 5.2 of PD3AA[118] states:

> *When the court has decided that a vulnerable party, vulnerable witness or protected party should give evidence there shall be a "ground rules hearing" prior to any hearing at which evidence is to be heard, at which any necessary participation directions will be given-*
>
>   a) *as to the conduct of the advocates and the parties in respect of the evidence of that person, including the need to address the matters referred to in paragraphs 5.3 to 5.7, and*

---

[118] Family Procedure Rules 2010

> b) *to put any necessary support in place for that person. The ground rules hearing does not need to be a separate hearing to any other hearing in the proceedings.*

Paragraph 5.5 of PD3AA[119] also states:

> *In all cases in which it is proposed that a vulnerable party, vulnerable witness or protected party is to be cross-examined (whether before or during a hearing) the court must consider whether to make participation directions, including prescribing the manner in which the person is to be cross-examined. The court must consider whether to direct that-*
>
> a) *any questions that can be asked by one advocate should not be repeated by another without the permission of the court;*
>
> b) *questions or topics to be put in cross-examination should be agreed prior to the hearing;*
>
> c) *questions to be put in cross-examination should be put by one legal representative or advocate alone, or, if appropriate, by the judge; and*
>
> d) *the taking of evidence should be managed in any other way.*

For those representing the alleged victim of abuse, the ground rules hearing would be the opportune moment to draw the parameters of cross-examination and to try to limit the issues to that which is proportionate and not unduly prejudicial.[120] For instance, it may be submitted that questions about past sexual history, previous partners and so on are not to be put in cross-examination as they are prurient and bear no relevance to the issues in dispute[121], but such submissions need to be

---

[119] ibid.

[120] See also: r. 22.1, FPR 2010 on the power of the court to control evidence.

[121] In making these submissions, reference could be made to the President of the Family Division's '*The Family Court and Covid 19: The Road Ahead*', op. cit., in particular: "Parties appearing before the court should expect the issues to be limited only to those which it is necessary to determine to dispose of the case…"

raised pre-emptively. The ground rules hearing is the time for these sorts of issues to be debated and determined by the tribunal and is an essential preparatory step for the advocates and the judge.

A word of caution: if the judge dealing with the ground rules hearing is also the trial judge, beware of rehearsing evidence before them which you are seeking to exclude but ends up being admitted by default because the judge has already heard all about its contents.

Witness demeanour and memory

The trial judge should be provided with a clear warning about relying on witness demeanour or body language when assessing credibility. The law in respect of the consideration of demeanour is helpfully summarised by Leggatt LJ in the Court of Appeal's decision in *R (On the Application of SS (Sri Lanka)) v The Secretary of State for the Home Department.*[122] Leggatt LJ observed in that case that *"it has increasingly been recognised that it is usually unreliable and often dangerous to draw a conclusion from a witness's demeanour as to the likelihood that the witness is telling the truth."*[123] He noted that the *"reasons for distrusting reliance on demeanour are magnified where the witness is of a different nationality from the judge and is either speaking English as a foreign language or is giving evidence through an interpreter"*[124] and went on to warn that attaching significant weight to the impressions created by the demeanour of a witness *"risks making judgments which at best have no rational basis and at worst reflect conscious or unconscious biases or prejudices."*[125] He concluded that the only reliable way to assess truthfulness is to focus on the content of the testimony rather than on how it is given, and to consider whether it is consistent with other evidence and with known or probable facts.[126]

---

[122] [2018] EWCA Civ 1391

[123] Ibid., at para. 36

[124] ibid., at para. 37

[125] ibid., at para. 41

[126] ibid.

In assessing and weighing the impression which the court forms of a witness, the court should also keep in mind the observations of Macur J in *Re M (Children)*[127] that:

> "*any judge appraising witnesses in the emotionally charged atmosphere of a contested family dispute should warn themselves to guard against an assessment solely by virtue of their behaviour in the witness box and to expressly indicate that they have done so.*"

The court's attention should be drawn to the problems associated with memory. Leggatt J (as he then was) observed in *Gestmin SGPS v Credit Suisse ((UK) Ltd*[128] that "*[w]hile everyone knows that memory is fallible, I do not believe that the legal system has sufficiently absorbed the lessons of a century of psychological research into the nature of memory and the unreliability of eyewitness testimony.*"[129] He went on to conclude that the best approach for the judge to take in a commercial case (this case was heard in the Queen's Bench Division but the observations are still relevant for the Family Court) is to place little if any reliance on witnesses' recollections of what was said in meetings and conversations, and to base findings on what can be drawn from the documentary evidence and known or probable facts[130] (echoing language which he will later go on to use in respect of witness demeanour in *R(On the Application of SS (Sri Lanka)*). For Leggatt J, the value of oral evidence lies:

> "*largely… in the opportunity which cross-examination affords to subject the documentary record to critical scrutiny and to gauge the personality, motivations and working practices of a witness, rather than in testimony of what the witness recalls of particular conversations and events.*"[131]

---

[127] [2013] EWCA Civ 1147, at para. 12

[128] [2013] EWHC 3560, at paras. 15 to 22

[129] ibid., at para. 16

[130] ibid., at para. 22

[131] ibid.

In *Re A (A Child)*[132], King LJ provides an equally helpful reminder about the limits of memory:

> *"40. I do not seek in any way to undermine the importance of oral evidence in family cases, or the long-held view that judges at first instance have a significant advantage over the judges on appeal in having seen and heard the witnesses give evidence and be subjected to cross-examination (Piglowska v Piglowski [1999] WL 477307, [1999] 2 FLR 763 at 784). As Baker J said in in* Gloucestershire CC v RH and others *at [42], it is essential that the judge forms a view as to the credibility of each of the witnesses, to which end oral evidence will be of great importance in enabling the court to discover what occurred, and in assessing the reliability of the witness.*
>
> *"41. The court must, however, be mindful of the fallibility of memory and the pressures of giving evidence. The relative significance of oral and contemporaneous evidence will vary from case to case. What is important, as was highlighted in* Kogan, *is that the court assesses all the evidence in a manner suited to the case before it and does not inappropriately elevate one kind of evidence over another.*
>
> *"42. In the present case, the mother was giving evidence about an incident which had lasted only a few seconds seven years before, in circumstances where her recollection was taking place in the aftermath of unimaginably traumatic events. Those features alone would highlight the need for this critical evidence to be assessed in its proper place, alongside contemporaneous documentary evidence, and any evidence upon which undoubted, or probable, reliance could be placed."*

The relevance of criminal law concepts

One of the interesting aspects of *Re H-N & ors* relates to the relevance of criminal law concepts in family proceedings. The Court of Appeal endorsed the observations of McFarlane LJ in *Re R (Children) (Care*

---

[132] [2020] EWCA Civ 1230

Proceedings: Fact-finding Hearing)[133] that it is *"fundamentally wrong for the Family Court to be drawn into an analysis of factual evidence in proceedings relating to the welfare of children based upon criminal law principles and concepts."*[134]

The Court of Appeal noted that the two jurisdictions serve fundamentally different purposes: the purpose of the criminal law is prosecution of criminal behaviour and punishment; the purpose of the family law is to resolve private disputes between parents and family members, with the paramount consideration where children are concerned being the child's welfare.[135] The Family Court tries to find out what has happened, what that says about the risk to the child and to the parent who was the subject of any abusive behaviour, and what can be done to safeguard them in the future.

The Family Court may well be tasked with assessing whether something has happened that is capable of being a criminal offence. For example, a family judge may be invited to find that one party was violent towards the other party. However, the family judge should focus on determining what actually happened rather than whether, in the criminal law, what happened would amount to actual bodily harm or grievous bodily harm.[136]

In the appeal before HHJ Ahmed in *Re A (Domestic abuse: incorrect principles applied)*[137], he concluded that the first-instance judge fell into error by becoming drawn into criminal law concepts when considering an allegation of physical abuse by the mother against the father. The mother alleged that father took hold of her hand and broke it. HHJ Ahmed observed that:

> 17. *Deputy District Judge Watson identified a number of different kinds of assault and referred to the defence of self-defence. He went into*

---

[133] [2018] EWCA Civ 198

[134] ibid., at para. 67

[135] *Re H-N & ors*, op. cit., at para. 60

[136] ibid., at para. 72

[137] *Re A (Domestic abuse: incorrect principles applied)*, op. cit.

great detail about the criminal principles to be applied. These included the circumstances in which reasonable force could be used in self-defence if a person apprehends an imminent assault of them. He said: "...now, a criminal analysis has some merit, but it also is not the entire picture." He carried out such a criminal analysis. That is demonstrated by his reference to it not being necessary for a jury to weigh to a nicety the exact amount of force to be used in self-defence. Reading those passages of the Judgment as a whole, it appears that the judge imposed a criminal standard of proof upon the mother, despite saying that he was applying the standard of the balance of probabilities. That is shown in particular by his statement: "I do not find that the father was guilty of an assault on the mother." He adds "... We must look at this as being wider than just criminal liability". However, the judge failed to carry out a wider analysis than criminal principles would allow.

18. McFarlane LJ (as he then was) stated in a case where the father had killed the mother, R (Children) [2018] EWCA Civ 198:

   "Criminal law concepts should not be applied in family hearings. The purpose of the family tribunal is not to establish guilt or innocence but to establish the facts in as far as they are relevant to inform welfare decisions regarding the children. It may be important for the children to know whether the surviving parent's actions were reasonable, as well as the potential for future harm to them (whether physical, emotional or psychological) if that parent continued to be involved in their care. It will often be necessary to have a fact finding to determine those matters, but the language used to phrase the facts sought and the judgment should avoid direct reference to criminal law concepts or principles such as 'unreasonable force', 'loss of control' or 'self-defence'."

19. *It follows that criminal concepts such as the elements needed to establish guilt of a particular crime or a particular defence have neither relevance nor function within the family court process.*

The observations in *Re H-N & ors* and *Re A (Domestic abuse: incorrect principles applied)* make clear that advocates should be live to judges becoming drawn into criminal law concepts which do not have a place in the Family Court. Prior to judgment being handed down, it would be sensible to make this point in closing submissions to prevent the judge from falling into error when making their findings.

However, we make clear that some criminal law concepts *do* have a place in the Family Court, and have done for a long time. For instance, family judges routinely give themselves a *Lucas* direction in respect of the approach to be taken to lies[138], the plainest and most obvious example of the criminal law being imported into the family law.[139] The Court of Appeal in *Re H-N & ors* is not saying that *all* criminal law concepts should be banished from the family law sphere. What the Court of Appeal appears to be warning against is an unhelpful descent into strict definitions within the criminal law rather than a holistic, common-sense analysis of the parties' behaviour. The Court of Appeal observes:

> "71. ... *The Family court should be concerned to determine how the parties behaved and what they did with respect to each other and their children, rather than whether that behaviour does, or does not, come within the strict definition of 'rape', 'murder', 'manslaughter' or other serious crimes. Behaviour which falls short of establishing 'rape', for example, may nevertheless be profoundly abusive and should certainly not be ignored or met with a finding akin to 'not guilty' in the family context. For example in the context of the Family Court considering whether there has been a pattern of abusive behaviour, the border line as between 'consent' and 'submission' may be less significant than it*

---

[138] *R v Lucas* [1981] QB 720, at p724, paras. F to H. See also the guidance of Macur LJ in the recent case of *Re A, B and C (Children)* [2021] EWCA Civ 451, at para. 58, where she considers the *Lucas* direction in some detail and suggests that it would be good practice, when a Lucas direction is called for, to seek counsel's submissions to "*identify: (i) the deliberate lie(s) upon which they seek to rely; (ii) the significant issue to which it/they relate(s), and (iii) on what basis it can be determined that the only explanation for the lie(s) is guilty. The principles of the direction will remain the same, but they must be altered to the facts and circumstances of the witness before the court.*"

[139] See, for example: *H-C (Children)* [2016] EWCA Civ 136, at paras. 97 to 102; *Re M (Children)* [2013] EWCA Civ 388, at para. 7; and *Re A (A Child) (no 2)* [2011] EWCA Civ 12, at paras. 59 and 104

would be in the criminal trial of an allegation of rape or sexual assault."[140]

Another obvious example of looking to our sister criminal jurisdiction for guidance on the approach to be taken in the Family Court is in respect of the issue of consent. In *JH v MF*[141], Russell J made the following observations about the approach to be taken to serious sexual assault in family proceedings:

> *"46. The Court of Appeal has considered the issue of analysing factual findings based upon criminal law principles and concepts in* Re R (Children) (Care Proceedings: Fact Finding Hearings) *[2018] 1 WLR 1821 : [2018] 2 FLR 718, Sir Andrew McFarlane (P) found that as a matter of principle it was fundamentally wrong for the Family Court to be drawn into an analysis of what had happened through the prism of criminal principles and concepts as proceedings could "…easily become over-complicated and side-tracked from the central task of simply deciding what has happened and what is the best future course for a child". Nonetheless there are many cases where the approach taken in the criminal courts to the interpretation of facts and analysis of evidence has been considered both helpful to, and applicable, in family cases; in any event there should be congruence of approach in both the family and criminal jurisdictions which would require some knowledge and understanding of the relevant approach criminal law particularly where consent is an issue. Two years previously in Re H-C [2016] 4 WLR 85 Lord Justice McFarlane (as he then was) said* "I have taken the opportunity to refer to R v Lucas in the hope that a reminder of the relevant approach taken in the criminal jurisdiction will be of assistance generally in family cases." *It can be taken from this that approach applied in the criminal jurisdiction are of relevance in the Family Court and in family proceedings.*

> *"47. While a trial in the Family Court cannot, and must not, set out to replicate a trial or to apply, or seek to apply, Criminal Law or statute*

---

[140] *Re H-N & ors*, op. cit.

[141] op. cit.

it cannot be lawful or jurisprudentially apposite for the Family Court to apply wholly different concepts or to take an approach wholly at odds from that which applies in the criminal jurisdiction when it comes to deciding whether incidents involving sexual intercourse, whether vaginally penetrative or not, and other sexual acts including oral penetration, penetration by an object or in other form were non-consensual. Non-consensual sexual intercourse was considered lawful within a marriage until as late as 1992 (Cf. R [1992] 1 AC 599) it has not been lawful in any other sphere for generations. There is no principle that lack of consent must be demonstrated by physical resistance, this approach is wrong, family judges should not approach the issue of consent in respect of serious sexual assault in a manner so wholly at odds with that taken in the criminal jurisdiction (specifically the changes in place since SOA 2003 and subsequent amendments). Serious sexual assault, including penetrative assault, should be minimised as an example of coercive and controlling behaviour (itself a criminal offence) although such behaviour may form part of the subordination of a potential victim's will (see the guidance set out at paragraphs 19 and 20 above).

"48. *To consider the relevant approach to be taken reference should be made to the statutory provisions in respect of consent; s 74 of the Sexual Offences Act (SOA) 2003 provides that* "'Consent' (for the purposes of this Part – my parenthesis) a person consents if he agrees by choice, and has the freedom and capacity to make that choice." *There are circumstances in criminal law where there can be evidential or conclusive presumptions that the complainant did not consent set out in ss75 & 76 which, respectively, concern the use or threat of violence by the perpetrator and the use of deception; neither of which preclude reliance on s74 (Cf. Blackstone's B3.46 2020 ed.)*

"49. *To quote from* Blackstone's Criminal Practice *[2020 at B3.28] where the absence of consent is considered it is said* "the definition in s74 with its emphasis on free agreement, is designed to focus upon the complainant's autonomy. It highlights the fact that a complainant who simply freezes with no protest or resistance may nevertheless not be consenting. Violence or the threat of violence is not a necessary ingredient. To have the freedom to make a choice a person must be free from physical pressure, but it remains a matter of fact for a jury as to what degree of coercion has to be exercised upon a person's mind before he or she is not agreeing by choice with the freedom to make that choice. Context is all-important." *There can be no reason why this approach should not be followed in the Family Court, whilst applying a different standard of proof. The deleterious and long-term effects on children of living within a home domestic abuse and violence, including serious sexual assault, has been accepted for some years, as is the effects on children's welfare, and their ability to form safe and healthy relationships as adults, if their parents or carers are themselves subjected to assault and harm.*

"50. In respect of consent in the criminal jurisdiction, which should inform the approach in the Family Court, the authors of Blackstone's *set out at B3.29* "Consent covers a range of behaviour from whole-hearted enthusiastic agreement to reluctant acquiescence. Context is critical. Where the prosecution allegation of absence of consent is based on lack of agreement without evidence of violence or threats of violence, there will be circumstances, particularly where there has been a consensual sexual relationship between the parties, where a jury will require assistance with distinguishing lack of consent from reluctant but free exercise of choice." *The Court of Appeal Criminal Division considered that a direction along the lines of the direction of Pill J approved in* Zafar *(Cf. the Crown Court Compendium (July 2019), chapter 20.4, para. 4) may well be appropriate. It should be advisable for Family Court judges to remind themselves of this approach and direct themselves appropriately based on the relevant approach contained in Chapter 20.*

"51. With further reference to B3.29 (Ibid) and the approach to take in making the distinction lack of consent from reluctant but free exercise of choice; "submission to a demand that a complainant feels unable to resist may in certain circumstances be consistent with reluctant acquiescence" *(Cf.* Watson *[2015] EWCA Crim 559); or where a complainant's free choice was overborne so that they did not have a free choice; an example of which was when a complainant gave*

into a perpetrator's demands because she was scared that if she did not he would have sex with her by force.

"52. As a further example of the approach to be taken in respect of consent in civil proceedings in Archbold Criminal Pleading and Evidence *2020, Chapter 20, Part II, at A [20-23] reference is made to the case of* Assange v Swedish Prosecution Authority *[2011] EWHC 2849 as* "relied on in R. (F.) v DPP [2013] EWHC 945 (Admin); [2013] 2 Cr App R 21, DC, for the proposition that 'choice' is crucial to the issue of 'consent'; and the evidence relating to 'choice' and the 'freedom' to make any particular choice must be approached in a broad common sense way; where, therefore, a woman consents to penetration on the clear understanding that the man will not ejaculate within her vagina, if, before penetration begins, the man has made up his mind that he will ejaculate before withdrawal, or even, because 'penetration is a continuing act from entry to withdrawal' (s.79(2) (§ 20-42)), decides, after penetration has commenced, that he will not withdraw before ejaculation, just because he deems the woman subservient to his control, she will have been deprived of choice relating to the crucial feature on which her original consent was based, and her consent will accordingly be negated."

"53. A further and instructive distinction between consent and submission and the approach to be followed was drawn in R v Kirk (Peter & Terence) *[2008] EWCA Crim 434: [2008] 3 WLUK 36, by Pill J at [92] where the expression "willing submission" had been used in directing the jury, it was said that the use of the expression was* "not an easy one in this context. Willingness is usually associated with consent. However, we are satisfied that the jury would not, in the context of this very full direction, have been misled by the use of the word "willing". This was not a case where it was alleged that submission had been achieved by physical force. It was willing in the sense that there was no attempt at physical resistance by the complainant and the judge used it in that sense. That leaves open the possibility that the circumstances were such that the complainant submitted to sexual intercourse rather than consented to it. That was the overall effect of the direction. We are

satisfied that, having regard to the full direction given, the jury would not have been misled or distracted, by the use of the expression "willing submission", from the question they were told they had to answer. It is not, however, an expression we would commend for use on other occasions."

> *"54. The judge in the instant case should have considered the likelihood that the Appellant had submitted to sexual intercourse; he singularly and comprehensively failed to do so instead employing obsolescent concepts concerning the issue of consent."*

In line with the observations of Russell J above, it would be prudent to invite the judge at the fact-finding hearing (where there are disputed allegations of a sexual nature) to direct themselves appropriately about the approach to be taken to consent, drawing on the approach taken in the criminal jurisdiction.

After the fact-finding hearing

At the conclusion of the fact-finding hearing, it is quite usual for a section 7 report to be directed, which is a report prepared by Cafcass or a local authority which sets out recommendations about the child arrangements moving forward. The next chapter will consider the scope of the section 7 report. At this stage, we would simply make the following suggestions.

It would be prudent to keep a careful, verbatim note of the fact-finding judgment (if the matter is before lay justices, they will provide their facts and reasons in writing anyway). The court can be invited to approve the note of the judgment and then it can be sent to the author of the section 7 report to enable them to be fully informed of the court's findings prior to commencing their enquiries. If the court directs that a transcript be prepared of the judgment, there may be some delay in this being received and so a note of the judgment can act as a suitable 'holding position' until then. The court cannot rely on the parties to relay accurately its findings to the author of the section 7 report. Paragraph 29 of PD12J requires the court to record its findings in writing in a Schedule to the order in any event, however it would assist the author of the section 7 report to have the full judgment so that the findings can be contextualised. To prevent delay, practitioners should send any approved note of the judgment to the author of the section 7 report directly.

Paragraph 22 of PD12J notes that where the court directs that there shall be a fact-finding hearing on the issue of domestic abuse, it will not usually request a section 7 report until after that hearing. However, it is open to the court to direct a section 7 report prior to the fact-finding hearing (with a view to the section 7 enquiries being completed after the fact-finding hearing has taken place). It may be sensible to consider this option rather than waiting for the fact-finding hearing to take place before a section 7 report is directed. It usually takes at least twelve weeks for a section 7 report to be completed (though during the pandemic, they are taking much longer). If the report is only directed after the fact-finding hearing, there will be at least a further three months of delay. There are enquiries that the author of the section 7 report can usefully begin carrying out prior to findings being made (for example, gathering information from the child's school, meeting the child, meeting the parents, and so on). Those enquiries can then be finalised after the court makes its findings.

There is an obvious risk to this sequence of events which is that the author of the section 7 report will be approaching their enquiries 'blind' rather than with a clear understanding of the factual matrix. However, this has to be balanced against the delay that would ensue if the report is not directed until the fact-finding hearing.

Checklist for the Fact-Finding Hearing

If issues of domestic abuse have been raised, have you considered the following?

- ☐ Are you competent to conduct the trial?

- ☐ How are the allegations to be presented, if not in a Scott Schedule?

- ☐ What supporting witness evidence or third-party evidence would assist the court in determining the disputed facts?

- ☐ What special measures are to be put in place for the fact-finding hearing? Is the hearing to be attended or remote?

- ☐ If any of the parties are unrepresented, how is it proposed that cross-examination of witnesses takes place?

- ☐ Has the judge, in making their findings, become drawn inappropriately into criminal law concepts?

- ☐ Has the judge's attention been drawn to or have they given themselves appropriate directions or warnings e.g. a *Lucas* direction, a direction in respect of the approach to be taken to consent, a warning in respect of witness demeanour/the fallibility of memory etc?

- ☐ Is there an approved note of the judgment which can be sent to Cafcass pending receipt of the transcript?

- ☐ Alongside a note of the judgment, have the findings been recorded in a Schedule to the order?

- ☐ Does a section 7 report need to be directed at the conclusion of the fact-finding hearing? Could this report have been directed at the FHDRA, with a view to its completion after the fact-finding hearing?

CHAPTER SIX

THE DISPUTE RESOLUTION APPOINTMENT (DRA)

The DRA follows the fact-finding hearing or, if the court has dispensed with a fact-finding hearing, the section 7 report or any risk assessment. PD12J at paragraphs 32 to 39 directs what should happen next in *"all cases where domestic violence or abuse has occurred"*. The final part of the chapter on fact-finding hearings deals with the possible directions, including those for further assessment, that the court may make at the close of the fact-finding hearing.

When should the DRA be fixed?

PD12J specifies that where the court fixes a fact-finding hearing, it must at the same time fix a DRA to follow.[142] This prevents 'drift', with a clear timetable being identified for the progress of the case. Unfortunately, this paragraph is seldom honoured with many courts reluctant to block out listing time with hearings which may end up being vacated because of the way in which a case evolves. Practitioners keen to prevent their cases being 'kicked into the long grass' should press the court to list the DRA when the fact-finding hearing is fixed and be prepared to refer the court to PD12J if they encounter any resistance.

Judicial continuity

Hearings should be arranged in a way that they are conducted by the same judge or, where possible, the same panel of justices (and if that is not possible, the same chairperson).[143] The logic for this was set out in the case of *Re B (Children)*[144] which we discussed in Chapter Two, where Baroness Hale observed that *"[m]uch useful information is likely to fall*

---

[142] Practice Direction 12J, op. cit., at para. 20

[143] ibid., at para. 31

[144] op. cit.

between the gaps"[145] when there is no judicial continuity. This principle of judicial continuity may be dispensed with where it would result in delay and the judge/chairperson is satisfied, for reasons *which must be recorded in writing* (a requirement which, anecdotally, we would again observe is seldom honoured), that the detriment to the welfare of the child would outweigh the detriment to the fair trial of the proceedings.[146] If judicial continuity simply cannot be maintained, practitioners should consider inviting the court to direct that a transcript be prepared of the fact-finding judgment; that the fact-find judge hand down a written judgment; or that the fact-find judge approves a written note of their judgment which has been prepared by one or more of the advocates. This would ensure that any new judge is fully appraised of the findings which have already been made and any broader judicial observations which may be relevant at the welfare stage.

What does the section 7 report need to include?

Where findings of domestic abuse have been made, the section 7 report (whether prepared by Cafcass or Children's Services) will need to cover:

- information about the facilities available locally (to include local domestic abuse support services) to assist any party or the child in cases where domestic abuse has occurred;[147]

- whether further assessments, such as social work, psychiatric, psychological or risk assessment of any party or the child is required;[148]

- whether an Activity Direction to a programme commissioned and approved by Cafcass, which is usually the Domestic Abuse Perpetrator Programme (DAPP), is required. Acceptance on a DAPP is subject to a suitability assessment by the service

---

[145] ibid., at para. 76

[146] Practice Direction 12J, op. cit., at para. 31

[147] ibid., at para. 32

[148] ibid., at para. 33

provider. Completion of a DAPP will take time (often in the region of many months) in order to achieve the aim of risk-reduction for the long-term benefit of the child and the parent with whom the child is living.[149]

- the child's wishes and feelings. The section 7 report author will meet with the child as part of their enquiries, unless otherwise directed or where it would be unhelpful because of the child's age. The child should be seen in a neutral place such as their school to prevent any suggestion of undue influence by either parent.

- whether the child needs separate representation and should be joined as a party to the proceedings.[150]

To ensure that these matters are covered in the section 7 report, advocates should make them explicit in the court order directing the section 7 report, rather than assuming that Cafcass will deal with these issues as a matter of course.

Children's Services will generally be the more appropriate agency to prepare section 7 reports where the child is the subject of a currently open case; the child was the subject of an open case prior to proceedings being issued; or the court application was made as a result of a recommendation by Children's Services or with its support. If the party who has alleged domestic abuse reported the abuse to Children's Services prior to proceedings, they may prefer for the local authority to prepare the section 7 report as they will have existing information on their case files about the allegations of domestic abuse, and a social worker who already knows the family. From the child's perspective, if there are existing workers who are known to them who could complete the section 7 report, this prevents the need for them to be introduced to yet another professional.

---

[149] ibid., at para. 34

[150] ibid., at para. 24. See also: FPR 2010, r. 16.4.

Can final orders be made at the DRA?

Where the parties agree to the recommendations within the section 7 report, the court may make a final order, including stepped arrangements, at the DRA provided it has considered paragraphs 35 to 39 of PD12J. The paragraphs are set out here for ease of reference:

35. *When deciding the issue of child arrangements the court should ensure that any order for contact will not expose the child to an unmanageable risk of harm and will be in the best interests of the child.*

36. *In the light of any findings of fact or admissions or where domestic abuse is otherwise established, the court should apply the individual matters in the welfare checklist with reference to the domestic abuse which has occurred and any expert risk assessment obtained. In particular, the court should in every case consider any harm which the child and the parent with whom the child is living has suffered as a consequence of that domestic abuse, and any harm which the child and the parent with whom the child is living is at risk of suffering, if a child arrangements order is made. The court should make an order for contact only if it is satisfied that the physical and emotional safety of the child and the parent with whom the child is living can, as far as possible, be secured before during and after contact, and that the parent with whom the child is living will not be subjected to further domestic abuse by the other parent.*

37. *In every case where a finding or admission of domestic abuse is made, or where domestic abuse is otherwise established, the court should consider the conduct of both parents towards each other and towards the child and the impact of the same. In particular, the court should consider –*

    a. *the effect of the domestic abuse on the child and on the arrangements for where the child is living;*

    b. *the effect of the domestic abuse on the child and its effect on the child's relationship with the parents;*

THE FACT-FINDING HEARING

  c. *whether the parent is motivated by a desire to promote the best interests of the child or is using the process to continue a form of domestic abuse against the other parent;*

  d. *the likely behaviour during contact of the parent against whom findings are made and its effect on the child; and*

  e. *the capacity of the parents to appreciate the effect of past domestic abuse and the potential for future domestic abuse.*

38. *Where any domestic abuse has occurred but the court, having considered any expert risk assessment and having applied the welfare checklist, nonetheless considers that direct contact is safe and beneficial for the child, the court should consider what, if any, directions or conditions are required to enable the order to be carried into effect and in particular should consider –*

  a. *whether or not contact should be supervised, and if so, where and by whom;*

  b. *whether to impose any conditions to be complied with by the party in whose favour the order for contact has been made and if so, the nature of those conditions, for example by way of seeking intervention (subject to any necessary consent);*

  c. *whether such contact should be for a specified period or should contain provisions which are to have effect for a specified period; and*

  d. *whether it will be necessary, in the child's best interests, to review the operation of the order; if so the court should set a date for the review consistent with the timetable for the child, and must give directions to ensure that at the review the court has full information about the operation of the order.*

  Where a risk assessment has concluded that a parent poses a risk to a child or to the other parent, contact via a supported contact centre, or contact supervised by a parent or relative, is not appropriate.

39. *Where the court does not consider direct contact to be appropriate, it must consider whether it is safe and beneficial for the child to make an order for indirect contact.*

There are a few points we would draw out from the above paragraphs.

Firstly, paragraph 37(c) of PD12J requires the court to consider, in every case where domestic abuse has been established, whether one parent is using the court process to continue a form of domestic abuse against the other parent. Practitioners should be ready to bring to the court's attention any litigation conduct which, in circumstances where domestic abuse is not an issue, may seem unremarkable. For instance, if a party does not comply with directions; attend court hearings; or keep the other party appraised of any developments which will impact the progression of the case – these might seem like "minor" non-compliance issues which can be overlooked and forgiven, particularly if the party is representing themselves and is not familiar with court procedure. However, this could also be a mechanism by which that party is needlessly prolonging the proceedings in order to continue their abusive behaviour towards the other party. While some judges will be sympathetic to litigants-in-person and willing to give them the benefit of the doubt when their unhelpful litigation conduct negatively impacts the court proceedings; advocates should be prepared to draw the tribunal's attention to the more sinister implications of this behaviour on the party who has suffered abuse. It will be extremely traumatic for a victim of abuse to be hauled into court for hearing after hearing only to find that matters have not and cannot move forward because of a lack of engagement in the proceedings by the abusive party.

Secondly, PD12J makes clear that where a risk assessment concludes that a parent poses a risk to a child or to the other parent, supported contact or contact supervised by a parent or a relative is *not* appropriate. This is significant to note because the use of the words "*is not appropriate*" makes this a mandatory requirement rather than a matter for the court's discretion. As a result, it seems that no matter what the *degree* of risk or what the *nature* of the risk, if the section 7 report or other risk assessment concludes that there *is* a risk, then there must be at least professionally supervised contact (probably in a contact centre).

This raises the question of what a parent who has been identified as a risk must do in order to progress their contact from supervised to unsupervised. Does there need to be further risk assessment which positively concludes that they are no longer a risk? Could the DAPP final report (considered below) be taken into account by the court in lieu of a further risk assessment?

What seems to follow is that it would not be appropriate for the court to specify a certain amount of work to be completed or a certain period of time that can elapse before contact can be automatically progressed. Risk is fluid and will need ongoing, independent assessment, with the oversight of the court. The court cannot be confident that if certain boxes are ticked, the risk will be removed. Advocates acting for the party who suffered the domestic abuse should resist the making of final orders with stepped arrangements for the progress of contact from supervised to unsupervised. Either the court needs to keep the matter in proceedings and list the case for a review hearing after work has been completed by the abuser and further risk assessment has been carried out (as suggested at para. 38(d) of PD12J, set out above); or it should conclude with final orders specifying child arrangements that cannot go further than professionally supervised contact.

The Domestic Abuse Perpetrator Programme

While Cafcass and the court may take the view that a party against whom findings have been made needs to attend a DAPP, many DAPPs have strict eligibility criteria which demand that any participant accepts some degree of responsibility for their abusive behaviour. If a party disputes outright that they have acted in an abusive manner and rejects the findings of the court, it is highly unlikely that a DAPP will accept them onto the programme.

If a DAPP is directed and the person against whom findings have been made is accepted onto the course, it is likely the court will wish to have sight of the halfway and final report from the DAPP provider before making any final orders as to their contact. In those scenarios, a further directions hearing after the DRA will be required at which the way forward will be reconsidered in light of the progress made. Ideally, the issues could be narrowed and a final order made by agreement of the parties and the endorsement of the court. However, if child arrangements remain in dispute, the court may need to list a contested final hearing to see if any progress can be made in respect of contact, depending on what the DAPP provider feeds back to the court.

On 12th May 2021, Cafcass issued an update on their website, raising concerns about the adverse effect of the coronavirus pandemic on the provision of Domestic Abuse Perpetrator Programmes (DAPPs) in England and the resulting backlog of several hundreds of cases.[151] Cafcass issued, with immediate effect, temporary guidance to support its Family Court Advisers when making recommendations in the current context where DAPP provision is severely limited. That guidance was most recently reviewed on 7th June 2021.[152]

The guidance notes that:

- Careful thought has been given to remote DAPPs but the research base does not currently exist to supports its effectiveness.

- There will be some cases where it becomes impossible to progress safe contact arrangements in the absence of a DAPP.

- Where the Family Court Adviser's risk analysis indicates that future harm is manageable and a DAPP is desirable rather than essential, it may be defensible to progress without one. Recommendations, however, must be carefully risk-assessed.

---

[151] Cafcass, *'Current provision of Domestic Abuse Perpetrator Programmes'*, 12th May 2021, accessed at cafcass.gov.uk

[152] S. Parsons, *'Temporary practice guidance for staff, in the absence of Cafcass commissioned Domestic Abuse Perpetrator Programmes'*, reviewed on 7 June 2021, accessed at cafcass.gov.uk

- The guidance provides standard text to assist Family Court Advisers as follows:

> *The need for xxx to attend a DAPP has been considered. Cafcass commissioned Domestic Abuse Perpetrator Programmes (DAPPs) have been severely delayed by the pandemic. It is therefore important to make the court aware that if a DAPP is ordered there will be a significant delay in the referral being made to the provider of the programme and the programme commencing if assessed as suitable. This will inevitably impact on arrangements for the child. It is not possible to say with certainty how long this delay will be, but it will be in the order of a number of months. In these circumstances, careful consideration has been given to a) whether any alternative recommendation to a DAPP could meet the children's needs b) whether DAPP is the only available option to provide the opportunity for safe and beneficial time with the parent/carer attending the course, for the children.*

It is not clear for how long this guidance will be in place. As such, it would be wise for any direction for a section 7 report to make clear that if the author recommends a DAPP, they should also give recommendations for alternatives in the absence of a DAPP being available which meet Cafcass' minimum standards. This is to avoid the scenario of a parent self-funding an alternative to DAPP which cannot be endorsed by Cafcass or the court as an effective alternative.

Challenging a section 7 report

It is not uncommon for one or other party to disagree with the recommendations in the section 7 report. Perhaps the party alleging abuse considers that the author has minimised their concerns and the risk of harm to the child. Perhaps the party facing the allegations of abuse believes the author has overstated the risk of harm. Whatever the objection might be, if these disagreements cannot be resolved by negotiation or brief submissions at the DRA, the matter will need to be listed to a contested final hearing, with the author of the section 7 report attending to be cross-examined on the contents of their report.

A helpful tool for practitioners in assessing the quality of analysis in a section 7 report is Cafcass's own '*Practice Pathway: A structured approach to risk assessment of domestic abuse*'.[153] This provides a benchmark against which the section 7 report can be considered. The Pathway acts as a best practice document to assist family court advisers in planning and structuring their assessments in cases featuring domestic abuse. It invites the family court advisers to reflect on a wide range of prompts and questions such as: how can identity be promoted if no in-person arrangements are recommended with one parent? Could a bridging intervention help make contact safer? Is the voice of the child clearly visible in the report? The goal of the Pathway is to ensure that the Family Court Adviser provides a structured, evidence-based risk analysis, and it is a useful springboard from which to plan any cross-examination.

Checklist for the DRA

If issues of domestic abuse have been raised, have you considered the following?

☐ Was the DRA listed at the same time as the fact-finding hearing?

☐ Are all hearings listed before the same judge or chairperson of lay justices who dealt with the fact-finding hearing?

☐ If judicial continuity cannot be secured, is there a transcript, written judgment or approved note of the fact-finding judgment? Has the court recorded its reasons in writing why it has dispensed with the need for judicial continuity?

☐ Does the court order directing the section 7 report make explicit all the matters which the report needs to cover?

☐ Is there adequate evidence before the court at the DRA to make final orders which do not expose the child to unmanageable risk?

---

[153] Cafcass, '*Cafcass Domestic Abuse Practice Guidance: A structured approach to risk assessment of domestic abuse in the family court*', accessed at cafcass.gov.uk

☐ Has the section 7 report/risk assessment identified that one parent is a risk to a child or the other parent? If so, is a further review hearing required once the parent has engaged in work to reduce that risk?

☐ If a party has been required to attend a DAPP, is there a waiting list before they can complete the programme? If there is likely to be significant delay, is there an alternative to completing a DAPP which will reduce the identified risk?

☐ Does the matter need to be listed for a final hearing? What gaps are there in the section 7 report which need to be challenged at a final hearing?

CONCLUSION

We are conscious that the moment this book goes to print, it is likely that a flurry of new case law and guidance will emerge that may well challenge the observations we have made here. That is the nature of this particular area of law. It is fast-evolving, intensely political and highly emotive – but that is what makes it so very interesting.

The headline conclusion from the cases of *F v M* and *Re H-N & Ors* is that PD12J is *"fit for purpose"*. We would agree with that. In our view, the issue lies not with what PD12J says, but with how courts deploy it. For PD12J to be implemented effectively, we need not only courts and lawyers to be better informed about its contents, but we need a well-resourced family justice system which allows us to use it as intended. It is all well and good setting out in detailed paragraphs what courts must do, but if courts are not supported by the money and time to be able to put this into practice, then little progress is going to be made. As just one example: Sir James Munby, in conversation with Louise Tickle as part of her Dispatches documentary '*Torn Apart: Family Courts Uncovered*' was asked if he had a magic wand to improve the way the system deals with domestic abuse, what would he do? He responded: *"the answer is training; it's the only answer"*.[154] However, he went on to note that training is expensive and the Judicial College does not have the resources to train magistrates as well as full-time judges.

While we would be cautious about saying that *Re H-N & ors* or the Domestic Abuse Act 2021 will mark a sea-change in the family court's treatment of domestic abuse, we anticipate that we will see some patterns and some shifts in approach in the coming months and years. As we have already observed in this book, it is likely that the existing pressures on court time will only be exacerbated by the decision in *Re H-N & ors*. We think it likely that judges will be increasingly cautious about case managing matters too robustly or preventing parties from raising allegations for fear of opening themselves up to appeal. We are also going to see some experimentation and trial and error with different forms of

---

[154] L. Tickle, '*Torn Apart: Family Courts Uncovered: Dispatches*', op. cit.

presenting allegations, as we move away from Scott Schedules. For all the criticisms of Scott Schedules, there is no doubt that they did focus parties' minds. In the absence of Schedules, there is a risk of disproportionate multi-day fact-finding hearings being listed if parties are allowed, for example, to file lengthy narrative statements with no limit.

However, rather than re-hashing what we have already said elsewhere in this book, we wanted to use this final chapter to look at what may be on the horizon and what else we think is needed to move this area of law along.

As readers will now know, judicial training has been a recurring recommendation over the years, from Nicholas Wall in 2006[155] to the observations of Russell J in *JH v MF*.[156] Albeit the Court of Appeal in *Re H-N & ors* asserted confidently that the modern approach to domestic abuse "*has become embedded through training and experience in the practice of the vast majority of judges and magistrates sitting in the Family Court*"[157], the '*View from The President's Chambers: July 2021*' revealed that the Judicial College is developing new training covering the impact of the Domestic Abuse Act 2021 and the guidance given in *Re H-N & ors*. In addition, the College was working to refresh the current online training during the summer of 2021 and new seminars are being planned for the training programme in 2022 to 2023.[158]

However, this training is only accessible to members of the judiciary. There is an urgent need for training of a similar content to be made available to legal professionals, Cafcass officers and child social work practitioners. Barristers, solicitors and other legal professionals begin their careers with no formal training around domestic abuse. We are

---

[155] N. Wall, '*A report to the President of the Family Division on the publication by the Women's Aid Federation of England entitled Twenty-nine child homicides: lessons still to be learnt on domestic violence and child protection with particular reference to the five cases in which there was judicial involvement*', op. cit.

[156] *JH v MF*, op. cit.

[157] *Re H-N & ors*, op. cit., at para. 53

[158] A. McFarlane, '*View from the President's Chambers*', 12th July 2021, accessed at judiciary.uk

CONCLUSION

expected to learn on the jobs and to pick it up as we go. This is not good enough. The responsibility lies with us to hold judges accountable when they fall short in their treatment of domestic abuse. We cannot do this effectively if we do not know the standard to which we should hold them.

Off the back of the Harm Report and the work completed by the President's Private Law Working Group, the Ministry of Justice has prepared an implementation plan with a view to taking steps towards improving the experiences of victims of domestic abuse in the family courts. The most intriguing recommendation in this plan is the commitment to piloting the Integrated Domestic Abuse Court: "*a more integrated approach between different parts of the justice system*".[159] The plan notes that the pilot will explore two approaches.[160] The first will be a 'one family one judge' approach in which concurrent family and criminal proceedings involving domestic abuse will be heard by the same cross-ticketed judge, preventing the need for victims of domestic abuse to repeat their trauma to different people and encouraging an end to silo-working. The second will explore an 'investigative' approach, moving away from adversarial system we currently have in place. Both approaches are reminiscent of the Family Drug and Alcohol Court, which we know has had some extremely positive outcomes.[161] It is not clear when these pilots will come to fruition and the implementation plan states that the start date will be dependent on the duration and impact of the Covid-19 pandemic (which does raise the concern that – as with many ambitious plans – these initiatives will become lost during the passing of time).

We have thought long and hard about how we wish to end this book, and we have identified three matters that we hope will leave readers with food for thought.

First, we would hope that there is an increased push towards publication of judgments and transparency in the Family Court when it comes to this

---

[159] Ministry of Justice, '*Assessing Risk of Harm to Children and Parents in Private Law Children Cases – Implementation Plan*', 2020, at p5, accessed at gov.uk

[160] ibid., at p7

[161] J. Harwin et al., '*After FDAC: outcomes 5 years later – Final Report*', December 2016, Lancaster University, accessed at wp.lancs.ac.uk/cfj-fdac/publications

kind of work. The bulk of private law children work is dealt with by lay justices, deputy district judges, district judges, circuit judges and recorders. However, judgments are not routinely published at this level and important decisions which will have a huge impact on the lives of parents and children often take place behind closed doors. Usually, we only hear about what is going on inside the Family Court when something goes horribly wrong (as was the case in *Re H-N & ors*). This is not conducive to building trust between the family justice system and the general public. Judges should more readily 'show their working out' and advocates should be more willing to place pressure on judges to do so. This is one of the key ways that the family justice system can counter the damaging narrative of the sinister, secret Family Court. A system is only as effective as the trust its users place in it.

Second, we hope that the judgment in *Re H-N & ors* and the emerging case law since then will encourage practitioners to be more ready and willing to challenge non-compliance with PD12J and to seek permission to appeal if domestic abuse has not been addressed robustly. The President of the Family Division in *Re H-N & ors* observed that: "*[t]he combination of the detailed guidance in PD12J together with the training in place for those judges who try these cases means that despite the high volume of cases, the number of appeals in private law children cases is small...*" It may be the case that judicial training and guidance is the reason why there are so few appeals; equally, it could be because non-compliance with PD12J is not challenged frequently enough. Meaningful change will only be effected if practitioners are willing to put their heads above the parapet to call out poor practice.

Finally, this area of law, as with much of family law, is closely intertwined with what is going on *outside* the courts in civil society. Family law does not exist in a vacuum, and many of the difficulties which the family courts are tasked with resolving could have been addressed long before these cases ever came anywhere near a judge.

As we noted in our introductory chapter, in the last year, about 40% (22,000 of 55,253) of private law cases involved allegations of domestic abuse. The 40% statistic is indicative of an endemic social problem which needs addressing at a much earlier stage. PD12J is a reactive framework which looks at how courts are to respond to keep children and victims safe when they have already suffered the ills of domestic abuse; it does not tackle the causes. If we are to address the "*scourge*" of domestic abuse, as Sir James Munby referred to it, far more needs to be done at a societal and governmental level.

Healthy relationship work and initiatives around identifying domestic abuse must be taught to children in school. Schools must create an environment which makes clear that abusive behaviours – which may manifest in many ways – will not be tolerated. Teachers and parents should receive training on spotting the signs of domestic abuse. Victims of domestic abuse, particularly children, need to be able to access therapy to process what they have experienced so that cycles of abusive behaviour can be broken. More resources need to be directed towards local authorities, domestic abuse charities and refuges so that victims of domestic abuse can access the support that they need to keep themselves and their children safe. All these measures, and more, are needed to prevent systemic and long-term overwhelm of the Family Court. What we do within the family justice system is just one small piece of a far bigger jigsaw.

MORE BOOKS BY LAW BRIEF PUBLISHING

A selection of our other titles available now:-

'A Practical Guide to Solicitor and Client Costs – 2nd Edition' by Robin Dunne
'Constructive Dismissal – Practice Pointers and Principles' by Benjimin Burgher
'A Practical Guide to Religion and Belief Discrimination Claims in the Workplace' by Kashif Ali
'A Practical Guide to the Law of Medical Treatment Decisions' by Ben Troke
'Fundamental Dishonesty and QOCS in Personal Injury Proceedings: Law and Practice' by Jake Rowley
'A Practical Guide to the Law in Relation to School Exclusions' by Charlotte Hadfield & Alice de Coverley
'A Practical Guide to Divorce for the Silver Separators' by Karin Walker
'The Right to be Forgotten – The Law and Practical Issues' by Melissa Stock
'A Practical Guide to Planning Law and Rights of Way in National Parks, the Broads and AONBs' by James Maurici QC, James Neill et al
'A Practical Guide to Election Law' by Tom Tabori
'A Practical Guide to the Law in Relation to Surrogacy' by Andrew Powell
'A Practical Guide to Claims Arising from Fatal Accidents – 2nd Edition' by James Patience
'A Practical Guide to the Ownership of Employee Inventions – From Entitlement to Compensation' by James Tumbridge & Ashley Roughton
'A Practical Guide to Asbestos Claims' by Jonathan Owen & Gareth McAloon
'A Practical Guide to Stamp Duty Land Tax in England and Northern Ireland' by Suzanne O'Hara
'A Practical Guide to the Law of Farming Partnerships' by Philip Whitcomb

'Covid-19, Homeworking and the Law – The Essential Guide to Employment and GDPR Issues' by Forbes Solicitors
'Covid-19, Force Majeure and Frustration of Contracts – The Essential Guide' by Keith Markham
'Covid-19 and Criminal Law – The Essential Guide' by Ramya Nagesh
'Covid-19 and Family Law in England and Wales – The Essential Guide' by Safda Mahmood
'A Practical Guide to the Law of Unlawful Eviction and Harassment – 2nd Edition' by Stephanie Lovegrove
'Covid-19, Residential Property, Equity Release and Enfranchisement – The Essential Guide' by Paul Sams and Louise Uphill
'Covid-19, Brexit and the Law of Commercial Leases – The Essential Guide' by Mark Shelton
'A Practical Guide to Costs in Personal Injury Claims – 2nd Edition' by Matthew Hoe
'A Practical Guide to the General Data Protection Regulation (GDPR) – 2nd Edition' by Keith Markham
'Ellis on Credit Hire – Sixth Edition' by Aidan Ellis & Tim Kevan
'A Practical Guide to Working with Litigants in Person and McKenzie Friends in Family Cases' by Stuart Barlow
'Protecting Unregistered Brands: A Practical Guide to the Law of Passing Off' by Lorna Brazell
'A Practical Guide to Secondary Liability and Joint Enterprise Post-Jogee' by Joanne Cecil & James Mehigan
'A Practical Guide to the Pre-Action RTA Claims Protocol for Personal Injury Lawyers' by Antonia Ford
'A Practical Guide to Neighbour Disputes and the Law' by Alexander Walsh
'A Practical Guide to Forfeiture of Leases' by Mark Shelton
'A Practical Guide to Coercive Control for Legal Practitioners and Victims' by Rachel Horman

'A Practical Guide to Rights Over Airspace and Subsoil' by Daniel Gatty
'Tackling Disclosure in the Criminal Courts – A Practitioner's Guide' by Narita Bahra QC & Don Ramble
'A Practical Guide to the Law of Driverless Cars – Second Edition' by Alex Glassbrook, Emma Northey & Scarlett Milligan
'A Practical Guide to TOLATA Claims' by Greg Williams
'Artificial Intelligence – The Practical Legal Issues' by John Buyers
'A Practical Guide to the Law of Prescription in Scotland' by Andrew Foyle
'A Practical Guide to the Construction and Rectification of Wills and Trust Instruments' by Edward Hewitt
'A Practical Guide to the Law of Bullying and Harassment in the Workplace' by Philip Hyland
'How to Be a Freelance Solicitor: A Practical Guide to the SRA-Regulated Freelance Solicitor Model' by Paul Bennett
'A Practical Guide to Prison Injury Claims' by Malcolm Johnson
'A Practical Guide to the Small Claims Track' by Dominic Bright
'A Practical Guide to Advising Clients at the Police Station' by Colin Stephen McKeown-Beaumont
'A Practical Guide to Antisocial Behaviour Injunctions' by Iain Wightwick
'Practical Mediation: A Guide for Mediators, Advocates, Advisers, Lawyers, and Students in Civil, Commercial, Business, Property, Workplace, and Employment Cases' by Jonathan Dingle with John Sephton
'The Mini-Pupillage Workbook' by David Boyle
'A Practical Guide to Crofting Law' by Brian Inkster
'A Practical Guide to Spousal Maintenance' by Liz Cowell
'A Practical Guide to the Law of Domain Names and Cybersquatting' by Andrew Clemson
'A Practical Guide to the Law of Gender Pay Gap Reporting' by Harini Iyengar

'A Practical Guide to the Rights of Grandparents in Children Proceedings' by Stuart Barlow
'NHS Whistleblowing and the Law' by Joseph England
'Employment Law and the Gig Economy' by Nigel Mackay & Annie Powell
'A Practical Guide to Noise Induced Hearing Loss (NIHL) Claims' by Andrew Mckie, Ian Skeate, Gareth McAloon
'An Introduction to Beauty Negligence Claims – A Practical Guide for the Personal Injury Practitioner' by Greg Almond
'Intercompany Agreements for Transfer Pricing Compliance' by Paul Sutton
'Zen and the Art of Mediation' by Martin Plowman
'A Practical Guide to the SRA Principles, Individual and Law Firm Codes of Conduct 2019 – What Every Law Firm Needs to Know' by Paul Bennett
'A Practical Guide to Adoption for Family Lawyers' by Graham Pegg
'A Practical Guide to Industrial Disease Claims' by Andrew Mckie & Ian Skeate
'A Practical Guide to Redundancy' by Philip Hyland
'A Practical Guide to Vicarious Liability' by Mariel Irvine
'A Practical Guide to Applications for Landlord's Consent and Variation of Leases' by Mark Shelton
'A Practical Guide to Relief from Sanctions Post-Mitchell and Denton' by Peter Causton
'A Practical Guide to Equity Release for Advisors' by Paul Sams
'A Practical Guide to the Law Relating to Food' by Ian Thomas
'A Practical Guide to Financial Services Claims' by Chris Hegarty
'The Law of Houses in Multiple Occupation: A Practical Guide to HMO Proceedings' by Julian Hunt
'A Practical Guide to Unlawful Eviction and Harassment' by Stephanie Lovegrove
'Occupiers, Highways and Defective Premises Claims: A Practical Guide Post-Jackson – 2nd Edition' by Andrew Mckie

'A Practical Guide to Financial Ombudsman Service Claims' by Adam Temple & Robert Scrivenor
'A Practical Guide to Advising Schools on Employment Law' by Jonathan Holden
'A Practical Guide to Running Housing Disrepair and Cavity Wall Claims: 2nd Edition' by Andrew Mckie & Ian Skeate
'A Practical Guide to Holiday Sickness Claims – 2nd Edition' by Andrew Mckie & Ian Skeate
'Arguments and Tactics for Personal Injury and Clinical Negligence Claims' by Dorian Williams
'A Practical Guide to Drone Law' by Rufus Ballaster, Andrew Firman, Eleanor Clot
'A Practical Guide to Compliance for Personal Injury Firms Working With Claims Management Companies' by Paul Bennett
'A Practical Guide to Dog Law for Owners and Others' by Andrea Pitt
'RTA Allegations of Fraud in a Post-Jackson Era: The Handbook – 2nd Edition' by Andrew Mckie
'RTA Personal Injury Claims: A Practical Guide Post-Jackson' by Andrew Mckie
'On Experts: CPR35 for Lawyers and Experts' by David Boyle
'An Introduction to Personal Injury Law' by David Boyle
'A Practical Guide to Subtle Brain Injury Claims' by Pankaj Madan

These books and more are available to order online direct from the publisher at www.lawbriefpublishing.com, where you can also read free sample chapters. For any queries, contact us on 0844 587 2383 or mail@lawbriefpublishing.com.

Our books are also usually in stock at www.amazon.co.uk with free next day delivery for Prime members, and at good legal bookshops such as Wildy & Sons.

We are regularly launching new books in our series of practical day-to-day practitioners' guides. Visit our website and join our free newsletter to be kept informed and to receive special offers, free chapters, etc.

You can also follow us on Twitter at www.twitter.com/lawbriefpub.

www.ingramcontent.com/pod-product-compliance
Ingram Content Group UK Ltd.
Pitfield, Milton Keynes, MK11 3LW, UK
UKHW022050090725
460558UK00019B/56